THLEWIAZA-SEAL RIVERS:
Challenge of the Ice
A Canoeing Adventure in the Far North of Canada

FRED E. NELSON

THLEWIAZA-SEAL RIVERS: Challenge of the Ice
Copyright © 2022 by Fred E. Nelson

ISBN:	Paperback:	978-1639455102
	Hardcover:	978-1639455119
	Ebook:	978-1639455126

All rights reserved. No part of this publication may be reproduced, distributed, or transmitted in any form or by any means, including photocopying, recording, or other electronic or mechanical methods, without the prior written permission of the publisher, except in the case brief quotations embodied in critical reviews and other noncommercial uses permitted by copyright law.

The views expressed in this book are solely those of the author and do not necessarily reflect the views of the publisher, and the publisher hereby disclaims any responsibility for them.

Writers' Branding 1 800-608-6550
www.writersbranding.com
orders@writersbranding.com

"Challenge of the Ice"

The lights went out! They just grew dimmer faded and went out! The cold and fatigue crept back into my mind. Despair and uncertainty gripped the six of us as we made our way across Hudson Bay to the city of Churchill on the south shore. It is 0200 in the morning, stormy, windy, very cold and raining as we fight to maintain control of our three canoes in four to six foot waves. During the previous 40 minutes our spirits had been raised, the cold and fatigue forgotten as we had our objective in sight – the lights – these we presumed were the lights of Churchill.

The ordeal on the Bay began at 2115 the previous evening, now we wonder just what it was we had been following the past 40 minutes. Once again fear gains the upper hand as we realize the tenuous position of our three canoes lost somewhere in the icy water of lower Hudson Bay on a stormy night.

How we got into this predicament and what happened in the next 12 hours is the culmination of a wild river canoe trip that started three weeks ago and some 470 miles west of our current location.

**IN MEMORY OF
GARY GNAUCK
AND
BRIAN GNAUCK**

River boots

Contents

Chapter 1: Meet the Canoeists 1
Chapter 2: The Beginning 5
    December 1977
Chapter 3: Rendezvous 9
    15 June 1978
Chapter 4: Lynn Lake 13
    18 June 1978
Chapter 5: Snyder Lake 17
    Day 1: 19 June 1978
Chapter 6: Getting Organized 23
    Day 2: 20 June 1978
Chapter 7: Kasmere Falls 29
    Day 3: 21 June 1978
Chapter 8: Kasmere Lake 37
    Day 4: 22 June 1978
Chapter 9: Life & Death Struggle 45
    Day 5: 23 June 1978
Chapter 10: Nueltin Lake 49
    Day 6: 24 June 1978
Chapter 11: Rest, Then South 55
    Day 7: 25 June 1978
Chapter 12: 29 Mile Day 61
    Day 8: 26 June 1978
Chapter 13: Surprises 63

Day 9: 27 June 1978
Chapter 14: North Seal River 69
Day 10: 28 June 1978
Chapter 15: Lost Gear 73
Day 11: 29 June 1978
Chapter 16: News of a Friend 75
Day 12: 30 June 1978
Chapter 17: Stoney Lake.. 79
Day 13: 1 July 1978
Chapter 18: Shethanie Lake 83
Day 14: 2 July 1978
Chapter 19: Cold! Wind! Fog! Drizzle! 87
Day 15: 3 July 1978
Chapter 20: A Continuation 91
Day 16: 4 July 1978
Chapter 21: Tundra... 95
Day 17: 5 July 1978
Chapter 22: Hudson Bay 97
Day 18: 6 July 1978
Chapter 23: The Ordeal 103
Day 19 and 20: 7-8 July 1978
Chapter 24: Return and Reflection 115
Day 21: 9 July 1978
Epilogue: Closing Comments by the Author, Fred E. Nelson... 119
November 2020

Chapter 1

Meet the Canoeists

CANOE: 17'Grumman, NAME: Wakemaker II

Gary Gnauck, San Jose, CA - Stern   *Greg Dufeck, Stacy, MN - Bow*

    Gary had spent many days canoeing in his forty years. This included extensive experience with the state of Minnesota Conservation Department during the summers while attending the university. He loved whitewater, but since he'd moved to California some ten years before this trip, most of his canoeing had been on slow, lazy rivers and tidal flats in the San Francisco area. His work as a resource scientist put him into backcountry on occasion, so he knew his way around the woods. In spite of this, he'd never experienced a wilderness canoe trip of the extent and rigors of the one we were about to undertake. The thought of six-foot-high standing waves, hidden boulders, jagged rocks, and fast water gave him some trepidation. In spite of his experience, he was the "novice" of the party, a strange and uncomfortable feeling.

Greg was twenty-five years old, weighed about 180 pounds, and was in good physical condition. He had been into serious whitewater canoeing only in the past several years, but during this time, he'd run many of the rivers in central Minnesota and Wisconsin. In 1976, he joined Brian on the Dubawnt River in Canada some four hundred miles north of the Thlewiaza River.

CANOE: 17'Grumman, NAME: H.M.S. Victory

Fred Nelson, Beavercreek, OH - Stern

Chuck Nelson, Beavercreek, OH - Bow

Fred and a friend, Dale Graff, had gone on their first wilderness canoe trip in 1969 with two others. Fred and Dale fell in love with the adventure, but the other two expressed the extreme opposite by saying they never wanted to take another wilderness canoe trip. Fred organized a canoe trip on the Harricana River in 1970 and was joined by Brian, Carl, Dale, and two others. Except for Fred and Dale, this was their first wilderness canoe trip. Fred, Brian, Dale, and Carl enjoyed these trips so much that they went on many trips together over the subsequent years. Brian became so enthused about wilderness canoeing that he planned a trip in 1971 and a trip every subsequent year.

The other two who went on the Harricana River trip had a completely different view about wilderness canoeing. Four days into the trip, the group came upon a very new, small town built to support copper mining operations in the area. These two said they had enough of wilderness canoeing and left the group to return home.

Chuck was Fred's son. One of the many things Fred learned on the Harricana River trip was to take whitewater canoe lessons. Chuck was delighted to take the lessons as Fred's bowman. As a result, Chuck became an excellent canoeist, as good if not better than his dad. Chuck was Fred's bowman on the Coppermine River trip in 1976 when they paddled to the Arctic Ocean.

CANOE: 17'Grumman, NAME: Harricana VI

Brian Gnauck, Marquette, MI - Stern   Carl Schmieder, Dayton, OH - Bow

Brian fell in love with wilderness canoeing on the Harricana River trip and organized a trip every year since. No one can read the river or plan a trip as well as Brian. Although he was already a very good canoeist when he went on the Harricana River trip, he also took several whitewater canoe-classes.

Although Carl loved canoeing and whitewater, his greatest joy was fishing, and the fishing along Canadian rivers is good to outstanding.

Chapter 2

The Beginning

December 1977

The story started in 1973, when Gary's brother, Brian, visited Gary at his home in San Jose, California. They made a pact to run a wild river together sometime within the coming seven years. Brian was a professor at Northern Michigan University in Marquette, Michigan. His summertime avocation since 1970 had been running wild rivers in the United States and Canada, when Fred invited him to join a group of canoeists who were planning to canoe the Harricana River in Quebec, Canada.

Detailed plans for the Thlewiaza River trip were hatched in December 1977, when Gary and Brian got together at their folks' home in Wausau, Wisconsin, for Christmas. Brian had already run several rivers in the Northwest Territories with Fred, and it was in this region that they looked for a suitable river. A "suitable" river was characterized by a remote wilderness location, whitewater, diverse environment and paddling conditions, good fishing, and an ending point near civilization. The last element provided for an easier return trip and also an opportunity to experience the people and culture of the far North Country. Another factor entered the river selection process. The year before, Brian and Gary's dad, Mr. Gnauck, had spent a week in Canada at a fly-in fishing camp. He'd had a terrific experience, and they thought it would be great to plan a trip where they could meet their dad and fish together.

Brian laid out his maps on the living room floor. They stretched over six feet in length. To one not familiar with traveling in the Lake Country of Northern Canada, the maps show only a confusion of many lakes and streams all jumbled together. These maps (at a scale of 1:250,000) are one of the most important items on a trip. Each canoe was to have a complete set; without them, navigating the North Country would be nearly impossible.

The search for the right river was quickly centered on the Thlewiaza River. The Thlewiaza begins at Snyder Lake in the northwestern corner of Manitoba, Canada; from there, the river proceeds east through a series of large lakes alternating with fast whitewater rapids. One hundred miles east of the origin, it drops into Nueltin Lake at Nahili Rapids. Treeline Lodge, a fly-in fishing camp operated by Bill Bennett, sits just two miles from the rapids on Nueltin Lake. Nueltin Lake is huge—over a hundred miles long—with many bays, numerous islands, and literally thousands of miles of shoreline. The lake is noted for its incredible fishing—grayling, great northern pike, and huge lake trout. Treeline Lodge is accessible only by airplane, or, if you're up to it, via canoe through one of the many rivers leading into Nueltin Lake.

Beginning at Nahili Rapids, the expanse of Nueltin Lake spreads northward, and the outlet of the Thlewiaza River is well into the Northwest Territories. The river proceeds east for another two hundred miles before dumping into Hudson Bay. The nearest point of civilization is the small village of Eskimo Point (presently named Arviat) on Hudson Bay, some fifty miles north of the termination of the Thlewiaza River.

Research on the Thlewiaza River revealed an interesting article published in *Outdoor Life* (January 1960). Two brothers began their trip at Nahili Rapids in the summer of 1954, traveled the Thlewiaza River to Hudson Bay, and then headed north to the village of Eskimo Point. Their trip took forty days; they got lost on Nueltin Lake, ran into ice, abandoned their canoe, and made the last twenty miles to Eskimo Point on foot. The extensive tidal flats on Hudson Bay, measuring two to seven miles at low tide, are very difficult to navigate.

Our plan was to begin at Snyder Lake, travel east 100 miles to Nueltin Lake, spend one day with Mr. Gnauck at Treeline Lodge fishing for big lakers, and then paddle the length of Nueltin Lake (a major milestone) to the outlet of the Thlewiaza River at Hudson Bay. From there, the plan was to turn north and paddle 50 miles to Eskimo Point. The total trip was estimated to be 450 miles. There was some concern about the last 50 miles. The extensive tidal flats, lack of fresh water, and unknown camping conditions would be a real test of our wilderness know-how. An additional worry was the very high concentration of polar bears in this part of Canada. Like the grizzly, the polar bear has no fear of humans; but unlike the grizzly, which typically ignores humans, the polar bear will often seek them out. A decision was made not to carry any weapons, as they are normally not needed; they are a heavy burden on portages and are generally not handy when you need them. In the previous nine years of running Canadian rivers, Brian had never had a need for a weapon. Gary was a little uneasy about this decision, yet he was free to bring one if he wanted; he simply chose not to.

Having made the decision to canoe the Thlewiaza River, Gary called his wife, Natalie; son Greg, seven; and daughter, Andrea, eleven, to tell them of the plan. They were in good spirits and wished Gary well, but Gary could tell by Natalie's voice that she had some reservation about him going into the wilds for a month. Brian's wife, Rebecca, better understood the situation, since Brian had gone on a wilderness canoe trip every year since going on the Harricana River with Fred in 1970.

Subsequently, Brian called Fred to see if he would like to go on the Thlewiaza River trip. Fred said he wanted to see if his son Chuck would like to go with him because Chuck had had an enjoyable trip on the Coppermine River with his dad, Brian, and three others in 1976. Chuck said the trip sounded great, so that made four. Brian called Carl Schmieder, who'd also gone on the Harricana River trip, to see if he would like to be Brian's bowman. Brian also called Greg Dufeck to see if he wanted to join the Thlewiaza River trip as Gary's bowman, and the answer was an enthusiastic yes.

Thus, we had a full crew of six, which is a good number for a wilderness canoe trip. Two people in one canoe would probably not survive if they encountered a major mishap such as their canoe being destroyed in a rapid or one person being seriously injured. Four people in two canoes would have a better chance of survival, but it would be very difficult. Six people in three canoes have a reasonably good chance of surviving a major mishap by having three people in a canoe and building rafts for food and supplies. The rafts could be towed behind the canoes.

Chapter 3

Rendezvous

15 June 1978

At last, after six months of planning, studying, and dreaming, we were finally on our way. Our destination was the Thlewiaza River in north central Canada.

Gary flew from San Jose, California, to Minneapolis-St. Paul International Airport on June 15, 1978, and then took a taxi to St. Paul and stayed with Irene Granovsky, his mother-in-law.

Gary got up early, put on the coffee, and took an early morning stroll before Irene woke up. She joined Gary for a second breakfast, and they had an enjoyable morning talking. Brian was due for lunch around noon. While waiting, Gary began the first of several packing and organizing tasks that dominated his time during the next eighteen hours. He repacked his Kelty Serac backpack from commercial air configuration to canoe configuration. A weigh-in on the bathroom scale showed only thirty-five pounds—not bad; but this didn't account for his share of food and those miscellaneous items that somehow always seem to be necessary.

Brian drove from Marquette, Michigan, to St. Paul and arrived as scheduled, just before noon. Irene put on an immense lunch spread, and all ate heartily. Irene was assured that the crew was very experienced and levelheaded; no one was going to take any unnecessary risks.

At 1315, Brian and Gary said their goodbyes and drove twenty miles north to the home of Greg Dufeck in the small town of Stacy, Minnesota. Brian and Gary grew up within thirty-five miles of Stacy. They knew the country well, having spent many hours in the vicinity hunting ruffed grouse, pheasants, and rabbits. Greg's home was designated the rendezvous point for this trip. Greg would paddle bow in Gary's canoe on the trip, and Gary looked forward to meeting him. Brian and Gary arrived right on time.

The early afternoon was spent unpacking and repacking. Brian brought the food for the entire party, but each man was to carry a portion. It took some doing, but Gary managed to get everything into his pack. Total weight —sixty-seven pounds, which was light; Brian's pack weighed in at seventy-eight pounds.

Life support systems minus canoe, tent and cooking gear for one person for one month

Mrs. Dufeck provided a splendid meal, which was quickly downed. After dinner, they talked with Greg's father. Gary was especially interested in the changes to Stacy and the surrounding countryside since he'd left this area some seventeen years ago. Then Greg suggested a quick paddle on the Sunrise River.

Brian and Gary jumped at the idea. The Sunrise River is a small stream with some nice rockdodging rapids. But at the point they put in, it was a lazy river that emptied into a large marsh area newly created by the Minnesota Department of Conservation as a waterfowl habitat. It felt good to dip the paddle deep into warm Minnesota waters.

Gary quickly discovered Greg's style of canoeing was different from his. Greg handled himself well and had excellent balance and a very powerful draw stroke. However, he liked to change sides often, whereas Gary typically paddled on one side for extended periods. Nonetheless, Gary was sure they would make a good team.

As darkness descended on the Minnesota countryside, they headed back to Greg's home. It was dark by the time they got back to Greg's house. Brian and Gary just made it to Brian's two-man tent they had set up in Greg's backyard before a summer rainstorm hit. By midnight, it was pouring rain, with considerable electrical activity. The tent remained dry, a good sign, as this kind of intense storm was not expected in Northern Canada.

Brian and Gary were up and about at 0600. It was clear and warm with no wind. At 0700, the remaining members of the party arrived. Fred, in his mid-forties, worked for the Air Force at Wright-Patterson Air Force Base in Dayton, Ohio. It was there, some eight years previous, that Brian and Fred had met. They both enjoyed camping, canoeing, and whitewater. Since then, they both had been down many Canadian rivers and had logged many miles of whitewater together. Fred was very thorough, methodical, well organized, and would command the HMS *Victory,* the red canoe. His bowman would be his son, Chuck. At seventeen, Chuck was the youngest member of the party but no stranger to a canoe or whitewater. In addition to the many day trips and weekenders in the Midwest, Chuck had joined Brian and crew to go down the Coppermine River in the Northwest Territories in 1976.

Carl Schmieder was in his late thirties. He was full of fun and could always see the comic elements in a serious situation (a trait that was to pay dividends later in the trip). Carl lived in Dayton, Ohio, and had known Brian and Fred for many years. Carl liked canoeing in the Canadian wilderness, not for the whitewater, which he tolerated, but, rather, for the incredible fishing these waters provide. To entice Carl to join him as his bow partner, Brian had promised Carl lots of fishing, including a full day on Nueltin Lake where the "lunker lakers" were to be the main objective. Brian and Carl would be cutting the northern waters in the *Harricana VI,* the blue canoe. Carl brought with him from Dayton the *Wakemaker II,* a green canoe. Greg and Gary would paddle this canoe, which had already seen action on many of the other rivers in Canada.

Mrs. Dufeck made breakfast for the six of us, and we consumed huge quantities of hotcakes, toast, and doughnuts and gallons of coffee. After breakfast, there was a flurry of activity as everyone completed personal packing, and we loaded up Brian's four-wheel drive Chevy wagon. It turned cloudy and began to rain as we finished loading the three canoes. We thanked the Dufeck for their hospitality and, at 1100 hours, left for a nonstop drive to Lynn Lake, Manitoba, some 1,200 miles away.

Day was just a continuation of the previous night as we drove through Canada. To keep the drivers fresh, we rotated every two hours. There was a place in the rear just large enough for someone to stretch out and get a good rest.

Driving along Lake Winnipeg, we entered the taiga from the prairie parkland to the South. One could not see much at this time of the morning, but the cool air with an unforgettable aroma, along with an unseen sixth sense, clearly established our presence in the North Country. Conversation was light, with many miles of quiet solitude, as each of us was lost in our own thoughts or catching some sleep. The hours and the miles drifted by as we headed deep into the Canadian wilderness.

A little after daybreak, we ate breakfast in Thompson and continued north on the last leg of our trip to Lynn Lake. We began to encounter some of the famous northern rivers, the Burntwood, Nelson, and Churchill. Brian and Fred had been down some of these rivers, and this sparked interest and enthusiasm. Conversation picked up, and the restlessness of the long ride permeated the car. We were all eager to get on the river. Enough planning, packing and riding; it was time now to get down to some serious paddling.

Finally, at 1405 on the eighteenth, we arrived at Lynn Lake. It was the farthest point north accessible by road. Our first task was to find Calm Air, the charter plane company that was to fly us to Snyder Lake. We felt, with luck, we could get to Snyder Lake today. It didn't get dark until 2200 or 2300, and Snyder Lake was only a one and a half-hour (184-mile) airplane ride away.

Chapter 4

Lynn Lake

18 June 1978

    Upon pulling into the Calm Air seaplane base we spotted our Twin Otter. It was not ready! The mechanics were just fitting the pontoons on the main fuselage, and it had not been flight-tested yet. Our hope of making it to Snyder Lake on schedule was dashed. This was the least of our troubles. We talked to the Calm Air owner and determined that we could fly out of Lynn Lake at 1430 the following day; however, he did not know if he could get us into Snyder Lake. The North Country was frozen in. Nueltin Lake was still frozen solid with three feet of ice, except right at Nahili Rapids.

    Back in town, we heard more and more stories and rumors. It had been the worst winter in forty years; Churchill River, Thlewiaza River, and all river systems to the north were frozen in, and the ice was not likely to break up on the big lakes for over a month. Additionally, we determined that Calm Air did not have an economical aircraft available to fly us back to Lynn Lake from Eskimo Point. As finances were limited, it was necessary that we make an arrangement with Parsons Air. They had a suitable airplane available but doubted that Eskimo Point would be open. We learned from the Parsons Air manager that the Thlewiaza River was breaking up between Snyder and Nueltin Lakes, but one could not get past Nueltin Lake.

    All of the foregoing brought about an intense and important planning session, as we needed to come up with contingency plans if we could not canoe the Thlewiaza River. The first alternative plan we dubbed "The Southern Cross." This plan cut due east across the south-central part of Nueltin Lake to an unnamed river system. This river system rejoined the Thlewiaza River at Edhorn Lake. The advantage was that 90 percent of Nueltin Lake, several other large lakes, and a major section of the river, all lying some one hundred miles to the north, would be bypassed. These areas would likely break up last. This would add a number of unplanned portages and some upstream paddling but was definitely feasible.

At this point, it wasn't clear that we would be able to make it to Nueltin Lake. The reality of the situation began to sink in. Our three canoes were helpless against ice. Even a few hundred yards would necessitate a portage, and if one of the large lakes was still frozen in or blocked with pack ice, our trip would come to a halt. We would have to wait for the ice to break up, which could be a day, a week, or longer. This would delay our arrival at the pickup point and probably initiate an air search, causing much worry and concern. Going back upstream to our starting point would not only be very difficult but also very unwise. The headwaters of the Thlewiaza are just under two hundred air miles from Lynn Lake, and no one would think to look for us in that area for over a month.

What if we couldn't even get into Snyder Lake? Then the plan was to fly from Lynn Lake to a lake near the headwaters of the North Seal. This would require getting a message to Mr. Gnauck at Treeline Lodge that we wouldn't be paddling the Thlewiaza River. Failure to get word to Mr. Gnauck would upset everyone back in the States with a month's worth of worry.

We checked in at the Royal Canadian Mounted Police and gave them our itinerary with a planned pickup at Eskimo Point. They asked if we were familiar with the North Country and clearly distinguished between the ability to paddle a canoe and knowledge of how to survive in the wilderness for a month. Brian briefed them on the experience of the crew, and they seemed satisfied. They wished us good luck and gave us directions to the local map distribution center. We made camp at Berge Lake on the outskirts of Lynn Lake. This was to be our most civilized campsite.

Berge Lake public campground near the village of Lynn Lake

After making camp and getting things organized, we strolled down to the lake and tested our fishing gear—no luck. A bit later, Greg decided a bath was in order. It was cold, 54°F; so it was a very short bath. Brian and Gary set up Brian's two-man Gerry tent. Fred brought his fourman Gerry tent; the other four were going to call it home for the next month. It had been a long haul; everyone was tired, and we turned in early. It was our first night in the North Country with a lot to occupy our minds, but sleep came easily and quickly.

Gary was up and out of the sack at 0500. It was cold, 34°F! Brian got up a bit later, and they woke the rest of the crew at 0600. By 0730, we broke camp and headed for a hearty breakfast in the village of Lynn Lake. We had a short, intense planning session that resulted in a decision to try for Snyder Lake and the Thlewiaza River in spite of the ice, hope for good weather during the next week, and reassess the entire situation at Nueltin Lake. If Snyder Lake was frozen, we would fly to the headwaters of the North Seal River and give the pilot a letter addressed to F. G. Gnauck, in care of Treeline Lodge, stating that we would be running a different river.

The next stop was the local general store to buy extra clothes. Gloves and towels seemed to be the most needed items. The map store was next. Unfortunately, the maps available did not have complete coverage of the Seal River system. We managed to pick up one additional 1:250,000-scale map of the North Seal. This still left a large section of the Seal River covered by a single 1:500,000- scale map and the last 170 miles of the trip, including about 40 miles of Hudson Bay, without any map coverage at all. This was not good news, but since the decision had been made to go for the Thlewiaza River, we were not overly concerned.

Our thoughts at this point were very mixed. It was exciting, demanding, and adventurous, and the spirit of moving boldly into the unknown prevailed. Yet we knew that 35°F to 40°F water temperatures were not to be taken lightly; a tip over could be serious. At this temperature, a person has only five to seven minutes to get out of the water, into dry clothes, and near a warming fire. Well, in a tip over, one cannot always get out of the water in seven minutes. Ten or fifteen minutes is typical. If the other two canoes cannot come to the rescue immediately, for whatever reason, it could be longer before one got out of the water. Knowing this, a silent fear crept into our minds—not awesome or overbearing but present nonetheless.

Chapter 5

Snyder Lake

Day 1: 19 June 1978

At 1400 hours, we checked in at Calm Air. The plane was ready; we could leave at 1430. The crew came alive with a flurry of activity. To add to our fortune, the pilot of the plane wanted to buy the canoes. Super! The plan all along was to sell them at Eskimo Point, as it was simply too costly to fly them back. We would get $150 for each canoe, but adjusting for US to Canadian exchange rates, this equaled only US$135. This was lower than what we wanted, as the canoes had cost US$150, but selling them now would save considerable hassle at journey's end.

Twin Otter returns from a successful test flight of our plane

The pilot, copilot, and the six of us loaded the twin otter. Three canoes, all our personal gear, and eight people fit inside the plane. It was a tight fit, but we made it.

Crew loaded gear into the Twin Otter.

Six canoeists, their gear, and three canoes all fit in the Twin Otter!

The plane taxied out; turned; and, with a roar of the engine, sliced through the choppy waves and into the air. We were excited, and every fiber of our being was tuned to the moment as we headed deeper into the North Country. Gary asked the pilot to tell him when we reached the edge of our first map. The bush pilots know this country well. They know

the location of Snyder Lake and how to get there, but Gary wanted to be convinced that we were on the right lake. He also wanted to become familiar with the general countryside. About an hour out, we encountered our first ice! Pack ice on one of the larger lakes. As we proceeded north, ice became more prevalent. Finally, on the horizon was Snyder Lake! There was a lot of pack ice present, but there were patches of open water as well.

Gary was taking pictures of the ice and was somewhat oblivious to the fact that everyone else was airsick or getting there quickly. It had been a noisy ride, but worse, raw gasoline fumes permeated the plane. Under any but these exciting circumstances, it would have been very bad indeed.

The pilot circled the lake several times and sat us down about a mile from the outlet of the Thlewiaza River. Thank God the river was open. We unloaded the aircraft quickly. As we loaded the gear into the canoes for the afternoon paddle, the plane taxied out into an open bay, took off directly overhead, banked to the left, and headed back to Lynn Lake.

The realization of being alone in the wilderness struck like a thunderbolt! This was it—no more abstractions, no more armchair canoeing; now we were on our own. Our success, our return to civilization, indeed our very lives was based solely on our ability not only to plan and execute the plan in the days ahead, but also on our foresight to anticipate and avoid problems.

Canoes loaded and organized, we shoved off at 1600. There was still considerable daylight left, and we hoped to make it to the first set of rapids some two miles ahead. Fred checked the water temperature in six-inch depth near shore. It was 40°F. Fred and Gary wanted to paddle over to the opposite shore to the ice  floes to take some pictures. Photos of the crew paddling along the edge of the ice would be spectacular, and in all likelihood, this would be the only ice we would see, as the lake was breaking up quickly.

Brian overruled, as he wanted to make some miles before the end of the day. We were already one day behind schedule. We could not resist trying out our fishing gear, and within five minutes, Carl landed a four-pound lake trout. Fresh fish for dinner!

We paddled on, found the outlet of the Thlewiaza River, and encountered the first marked rapids. Due to high water, it was drowned and presented little more than fast water and tricky current. It felt good to slice the water's surface and dig deep into the clear northern water. Gary mentioned that it was twenty years since he had been in the North Country, but the sounds, smells, and sights came back from his youth.

About four miles downstream, we encountered our first whitewater. We beached the canoes upstream and all piled out to look it over. It would be nice to have recorded the conversation of the "if, how, and where" we should run these rapids. The river took a sharp right turn at the rapids, with the main channel heading directly toward a large boulder. To miss the boulder would require a hard-right draw at just the right point; too soon and we'd crash into the rocks on the right shore; too late would surely mean hitting the center border, which would very likely cause a tip over.

Brian & Carl hit a rock, but made it through the rapids OK

Brian and Carl were first. Greg, Chuck, Fred, and Gary waited downstream just in case of a tip over. We were excited and scared; it was going to be tricky. We waited and saw the *Harricana VI* gain speed and shoot down the center channel. Brian and Carl held off a half second too long before they started their turn. They were being sucked toward the boulder as they commence a flurry of right draw stokes and fought hard to miss the boulder. We heard the bottom of the canoe hit rock, the canoe tipped to the right, but they passed without mishap and were grinning ear to ear as they paddled past.

Fred and Chuck were next. As the HMS *Victory* came into view, it was clear they had learned a lot about these rapids from watching Carl and Brian. They were much closer to the right shore and began their move earlier, slipping through with no trouble.

Now it was time for Greg and Gary. They were very nervous and excited. It was Gary's first whitewater in several years. It was not a big rapid, but it was tricky, and a tip over would not only be embarrassing but could also be serious. They climbed into the canoe, put on their life jackets, and secured the decking. They approached the rapids slowly and were quickly in the midst of churning whitewater. As they moved straight ahead, Gary reminded himself to wait, wait, not yet-- then yelled to Greg, "Right draw *now*, hit hard right!"

Greg's powerful draw immediately swung the bow to the right.

A split second later, Gary followed with a hard right to move the stern and instantly parry with a port side backstroke to straighten the canoe out and slow down.

"We made it! A piece of cake; knew it all along!"

By the time Greg and Gary navigated to the lower part of the rapids, which included going under a fallen birch tree, the others were well on the way to setting up the first camp. Chores were done, it was time for fishing. Carl and Gary paddled back  to the rapids. Within three minutes, Gary landed two graylings. Some fun! Working from the shore, Brian caught a northern pike, and Chuck landed a laker. Carl's laker back in Snyder Lake brought the total to five fish for the day, a result of about one man-hour of fishing.

Brian yelled to the crew "*Soup's on*" and all headed back to camp.

Dinner started with an appetizer of bearberries. Bearberry is a small herbaceous plant, the fruit of which winter over providing wildlife (in this case man) a spring treat. The berries are maroon in color, the size of peas and very, very tart. This was followed by cocktails (vodka or gin and dried mix) followed shortly thereafter by the main meal. In addition to the freeze-dried meal each man had several large pieces of grayling, northern and lake trout. To top it all off, there was raspberry cobbler for dessert. We were stuffed. If we were to eat this well for the rest of the trip, we will gain weight, not lose it.

After dinner, the conversation was mellow, and there was a contented aura around the campfire. Greg tried out his new rod and, within a few minutes, boosted the fish total to six by landing a six-pound laker.

To gain efficiency in the coming days, Brian made camp work assignments. Carl, Fred, and Chuck were to be tent men. Greg and Gary had the responsibility of gathering wood and getting the fire started for the three meals. (We did not know it then, but this was to have implications two weeks hence.) Brian was chief cook and bottle washer and, if this evening was any measure, a good one for sure. The latitude of camp was 50° 25', and at 2200 hours it was still quite light.

The days had a tendency to mask one's tiredness, and suddenly one realized how tired they were. Creeping into the sleeping bag made one feel that life was very good. There is an intrinsic value to the wild country; it was deeply inspiring to live in and experience it firsthand.

Chapter 6

Getting Organized

Day 2: 20 June 1978

Brian and Gary were up at 0400 and made the fire. Breakfast was excellent and again included fresh fish. We were eager to get under way; however, Greg and Gary had some difficulty in loading their canoe. It was clear they needed to establish a systematic approach to this task. As we shoved off, it was 0710; the *Wakemaker II* brought up the rear.

The morning was clear, and the air temperature was 35°F on departure. A light wind was on our back, a rare occurrence in canoeing. A well-known auxiliary of Murphy's Law (as it applies to canoeing) is, "One always proceeds with a headwind regardless of time or direction."

The first leg of our journey was in a northeasterly direction and quite short. The terrain was gently rolling and covered with a conifer forest consisting primarily of black spruce with scattered patches of white spruce. The forest was sparse, but the trees reached an acceptable size—30 to 40 feet high on average. Near the streams were birch and aspen. The brush, very dense at stream's edge, thinned out as one moved inland and consisted of Labrador tea, various willows, and some species that could not be identified. The ground cover was mostly lichen and mosses.

The first milestone was reached at 0930. As we turned due south, we saw clouds gathering in the southwestern sky. It looked like the clear morning was over. Our course took us almost directly into the wind as the sun disappeared and Murphy woke up. As we moved forward, gray clouds covered the sky and threatened rain.

Just then, we heard a terrible and unwanted sound. Coming low out of the northeastern sky was the sound of a helicopter. That was the last thing we wanted to see or hear. We did not journey over three thousand miles to be plagued by airplanes of any kind. It was clear that the chopper had business in the area. The pilot made several passes over us; moved toward the southwest; landed; and, a short while later, returned and headed east-northeast.

An hour later, the river suddenly constricted, and the current increased. The map showed a very sharp turn, and ahead we heard the familiar sound of whitewater. We approached slowly and cautiously. The river broke into several channels—two were very small and not navigable. The main channel was a boiling mass of whitewater with large rocks and boulders strewn throughout. We stopped to check it out. The rapids looked cold and dangerous. A consensus was quickly reached. This was our first portage.

As we unloaded the canoes, a cold, light drizzle began to fall. Gary immediately put on his Gore-Tex rain suit. Gore-Tex was a new material with billions of tiny pores that allowed passage of water vapor but not water droplets. When combined with nylon, it provided a waterproof but breathable garment.

Typically, some of the backpacks, canoes, and paddles were portaged first. The rest of the backpacks, camera gear and miscellaneous items were portaged on the second trip. No matter how one did it, a portage took two trips. Brian, Fred, and their partners were well organized and were coming back for their second trip while Gary and Greg were still struggling with their first load. A portage can be fun if it is done right. It provides a nice change of pace to padding, which at times became monotonous. On cold days, a portage can warm you up quickly. A portage improperly conceived and executed, however, can be a nightmare. Fortunately for Gary, Fred kept a sharp eye peeled. Gary met him about a third of the way back to get his second load and Fred said, "Gary, thought you might need this."

Gary looked; it was his map case!

The portage was short and wet, as the rain continued. The place where we put in was covered with dense trees and brushes. Reloading and shoving off took quite a while. It was hard work, but the Gore-Tex stood up well. There were no leaks, and it did not cause overheating.

As we proceeded downstream, it was quickly apparent that we were not through the rough water yet. The river was still swift, and very shortly, we came to the next set of rapids. They too looked ominous, but this was due more to the cold, dreary weather than an intrinsic quality of the rapids themselves. We decided to run them. The rapids were fun, and everyone was glad we did not have to undergo another portage.

Our spirits were dampened shortly thereafter, as we encountered another set of rapids— much more dangerous than those we portaged. The second portage was about a quarter of a mile long and was followed by a long paddle in open water exposed to the wind and rain. By noon, Greg and Chuck were miserably cold and had the shivers. We stopped on a nearby esker to have lunch. Greg and Gary made a huge warming fire and Brian set up a tarp. We sat down to hot pea soup, hot chocolate, bread, and jam.

After lunch, the river turned northeast, the low-pressure system moved southeast, and the rain stopped. It remained cloudy, and a cold, brisk wind set in, coming directly toward us out of the Northeast. Thank you, Murphy. The river opened up into Fort Hall Lake, the first of many big lakes we were to encounter. The wind gained a clear shot down the entire length of the river. Paddling was very difficult. Under these conditions, Gary realized that Greg's paddling style clashed too much with his. They were not making much progress. Greg took longer strokes and changed sides often, whereas Gary took shorter strokes and liked to paddle on one side for extended periods. This may sound like a trivial item to one who has not canoed for extended periods, but it could make a significant difference on a long trip such as this. A canoe is an extremely efficient vehicle if two people work together. If they don't, the canoe seems to drag and poke along no matter how hard one paddles.

An important compromise was reached. Greg shortened his stroke, and Gary agreed to change sides on Greg's cue. Within minutes, they had the headwind beaten and began to make good progress, the *Wakemaker II* slicing through the waves.

Fort Hall Lake was now behind, and we made it through a short, narrow river section into Thanout Lake, where we made camp at 1555.

Camp 2 was near Thanout Lake

Again, the newness of the circumstances left Gary behind the others in stowing his gear. Gary was still organizing his personal effects when the roar of our "friend", the helicopter, broke the concentration. We looked up just in time to see the large Sealand chopper land nearby.

All hurried over to where the chopper landed. We learned, talking to the pilot and three passengers who were geologists, that they were exploring for uranium ore deposits. This part of Canada had rich concentrations of ore, and if found here, it would change the face of the wilderness environment. The pilot also told us of a marked portage around Kasmere Falls, a major milestone we would encounter by noon tomorrow.

Sealand helicopter landed near camp.

Gary was a little put out by the helicopter's presence, yet he realized people had a job to do; and, taken in another light, the episode was interesting. Gary had once favored the establishment of wilderness areas. But in recent years, he'd backed away from advocating the lockup of additional wilderness areas. His work as a resource scientist brought him close to these issues, and he realized the wilderness simply served too few people. World food and energy demands required greater and greater quantities of natural resources. Intellectually, locking up land in a wilderness area was a luxury that we may not be able to afford. Here, in this part of Canada, there was no formal wilderness per se, just "original wilderness" undeveloped, open to whatever man's ingenuity would bring. At the moment, his emotions were very much in favor of preserving this land as it was for some future canoeist to explore and enjoy. We truly believed that, if all wilderness areas disappeared, mankind would have lost a "valuable resource," and with it would go a part of our collective soul. We came away from this meeting with mixed feelings.

The talk around the evening campfire brought out additional aspects of the problem. This was truly wild country, and the Canadian authorities were not presently equipped to handle large influxes of wilderness enthusiasts. The ecosystem here was very delicate, with low biomass turnover. Even careful, conscientious people could quickly damage the environment.

Even more to the point, it would be quite possible for some neophyte "wilderness expert" go from the States to Canada and get lost or killed. It is possible to foresee government bureaucracy in both countries piling regulation upon regulation regarding the use of the area. The next few years might be the last to enjoy this land with the ease and sense of freedom that this party enjoyed.

The day had been full and hard. We made nineteen miles and really felt good about that until Brian pointed out that we had to average twenty-three miles per day, and there were going to be several thirty-plus days ahead. That thought was overpowering.

Chapter 7

Kasmere Falls

Day 3: 21 June 1978

The day began at 0400; it was cold, clear, and very still, and a heavy frost hung from the branches. As the sun hit the trees tops, they burst into sparkling towers of diamonds. The scene would be common anywhere in the North Country in the winter—but not on June 21! Brian woke a short while later and, viewing the eerie, unreal scene, immediately pulled out his thermometer. It read 22°F! Incredible! Needless to say, we dressed fast and got a huge fire going. Breakfast was quick and breaking camp even quicker, although we lingered by the last remnants of the fire before finally beginning the morning paddle.

We shoved off at 0650. It was a beautiful morning—no wind, clear sky, and the temperature already 39°F and rising. Our pace at first was slow. Several complained that they were sore all over. The rigors of the previous day had taken its toll. Each stroke taken with the paddle awakened a new set of partially rested muscles. Within half an hour, the kinks were worked out, and all could enjoy the rest of the morning. We began to notice a few subtle but important changes in the countryside. The hills were higher, the trees taller and growing in denser patches. The eskers seem higher and better formed. All told, the country had a sharper definition.

The early morning paddle unfolded without any major event occurring. We encountered one small patch of snow on the shore just where a tributary joined the Thlewiaza River. This brought forth a volley of casts from everyone, each of us intent on catching the laker that was surely there; but low and behold, he wasn't home.

The river became deeper and smoothed out, and the current slackened. According to the map, ahead was Kasmere Falls and, beyond it, some three miles of associated rapids. The second hint that we were near the falls was an ominous dull roar, quite different from the "run-of-the-mill" rapids. A bit later, we saw the current pick up and the first part of the falls as it plunged out of view to the right.

Our first task was to find the "marked portage" the helicopter pilot had told us about. It would take us the rest of the day to portage the entire length of the rapids without a marked portage. An intense search on both sides of the river failed to reveal the portage trail, but it did bring some incredible views of the falls, and we had the opportunity to take good photographs. Brian had a great opportunity to get excellent whitewater shots with his 16 mm movie camera.

We held a council of war. The river took a sharp right turn and then gradually bent back to the left in about a one-mile arc, straightened out for a short stretch, and began another gentle left turn for a mile to a mile and a half. A decision was made to cross over to the north side, strike inland up over the hill, and intersect the river downstream at the end of the first left turn. The portage measured about three-quarters of a mile on the map. It was going to be a long, hard portage.

Brian led off at a brisk pace. The first one hundred yards were easy, and no one lost the pace, even though we went through a very difficult boulder field. At the end of a quarter mile, our party was strung out over fifty yards, with each canoe finding its own way through the woods. Gary's pack was heavy, and he was also carrying the cook kit and map case. He was beginning to feel the extra weight, which was slowing him down, and he was short of breath. He realized part of the problem was because he'd put on the wrong boots for this operation.

Organizing the gear after a long hard portage. The longest day of the year and there was still snow on the ground!

He explained later that he'd brought two pair of boots, both of which were waterproof. One pair was for heavy-duty hiking, ideal for portages and rocky country. However, he'd put on his rubber bottom / leather top boots, ideal for water work and walking in swampy marshland, but they did not provide the necessary support on long, rocky portages such as this. His feet were really taking a beating.

Poor Gary—when he thought he was at the halfway point, he found Brian and Greg coming back for their second load. Carl, Fred, and Chuck were nowhere to be seen, so he slowly continued. Each step was getting harder, but he felt moving was better than stopping. After reaching the ridge top, it was downhill on the other side. About three-quarters of the way down, there was a large patch of snow that followed a small stream to the Thlewiaza River. The snow was about three feet thick, frozen, and easy to walk on—except the surface was slippery due to melting.

We encountered substantial snow in the forest. June 21 and still snow; it was hard to believe. The put-in point was on the edge of the snow patch, which extended to the edge of the river. Brian, Greg, and Gary kibitzed and marveled at the snow. The other three fellows arrived, each by a somewhat different route. There was time-out for pictures before we went back for the canoes. Here the river was navigable, at least for the next half mile, which was all we could see. The walk back to the canoes without packs was delightful. We almost felt like running it was so easy (we didn't).

Coming back with the canoe was altogether another matter. The seventeen-foot standard Grumman weighs seventy-five pounds. The weight itself wasn't so bad; it was the proper balance that counted. Gary had not carried a canoe too often, so it was still intimidating. He described what it was like for him to portage a canoe as follows:

> Even with the yoke, the canoe digs into your shoulders. To rest your shoulder, you transfer more of the weight to your arms, and then the front end gets stuck in a tree and you can't turn the canoe because it is wedged in. You try to jam it forward in an attempt to bull your way through; in the process you lose your footing, a branch slaps your legs, the canoe is no longer balanced, and the front end begins to sag. You move your arms way forward and, using all your strength, bring the canoe back up, only to realize you can't get the damned monster through where you want so you have to back up. You can't see where you were going, and your foot falls in a hole; you just barely recover your balance when you realize your shoulder is throbbing once again. As you swing the bow around the bow rope comes off and gets snagged in a tree. At this point your partner is offering helpful advice like, "Hey, it looks pretty rough over there; why don't you try it over here?" Anyone want to attempt a portage?

Looking back up river toward Kasmere Falls, one get a sense of the general country-side and the extent of the snow.

By trading off every two hundred yards, Greg and Gary were able to make it without any major catastrophes and were glad the job was done!

After a thorough equipment check, we shoved off again on the icy cold water of the Thlewiaza River. The river was fast with small patches of turbulent water. These turbulent patches grew and merged into nice, runnable rapids. It was fun, exhilarating, and certainly beat the portage we just completed. Ahead, the rapids increased in fury; our excitement quickly evaporated and hopes for a full run were dashed.

There was a small break in the rapids, and we took advantage of the calm water to land the canoes. We got out and looked the situation over. Here the river began a second, long left turn and spawned a rock garden and boulder field. The water was too cold to chance a tip over so a portage was decided. The left side was low and marshy with solid brush. The right bank consisted of an esker several miles long and two hundred feet high. The lower elevation was dense forest and brush, but about midway up the esker, vegetation thinned out.

The plan was to climb the esker, follow it for a half mile, and then cut sharply left down through a marshy area and work our way out to the raging Thlewiaza somewhere near the end of the rapid. The first part of the portage was through brush, and going uphill was a bitch. The top stretch along the esker was relatively easy. The cut, down through the marsh, again presented a large block of rapidly melting "frozen snow." By the time we reached the river's edge, we were beat and on our last legs.

It took an hour for the crew to reassemble, and we all just collapsed. It was about 1400 and definitely time for lunch. This meal stood out as one of the most needed. Two portions of hot beef soup, two slices of bread with really thick globs of peanut butter and jam. The lunch conversation centered on the last two portages and the various incidents that had taken place. At one point near the end of the second portage, Chuck had taken a very bad fall as he stepped in a hole on the frozen snow patch. He was very fortunate that he had not pulled a hamstring or broken a leg. Carl, unlike the rest of the crew, did not work out before the trip and was not in top physical condition. It was clear he was on the ragged edge of handling the last portage. Fred too, was really beat. Working out for two and a half months prior to the trip, Gary was in fairly good shape but at his limit. Brian was in top physical condition and was probably not aware that the rest of us were exhausted.

After lunch, everyone was all in a satiated stupor. Excellent whitewater fishing was only three yards from the fire, and no one, not even Carl, even thought about wetting a line. Fred took the air temperature; it was 65°F. This was the only saving grace. If it was warmer, say 75 or 80°F, the past three miles would have closed out the day.

The thought of having to go back for the canoe was depressing. As we'd brought all the other equipment on the first trip, all that was left was the canoe, so Gary talked Greg into a two-man carry. Greg was reluctant, as he had never tried it before. A two-man carry in dense, rough country does not always work, and it is easier to get a canoe stuck or lose balance if the two people are not coordinated; but it is decidedly less total effort. Greg agreed to try, and was relieved, as he no longer had the strength or stamina to carry the canoe for more than one hundred yards without resting. The two-man carry was just what the doctor ordered, and they made it back; they were totally beat, but they made it.

Just as everyone was beginning to recover and felt that another hour of rest would keep us from dying, old slave driver Gnauck called out, "Up and at 'em, guys. We have a rapid to run and another six miles to go before we make camp!" Groans of disapproval filled the air, yet we all realized we had to push on. Getting behind schedule sometimes forced one to take chances. It was better to get ahead of schedule if possible. Then, if no problems arose, it would be possible to take it easy and really enjoy the subtle pleasures of a wilderness trip. With this understanding, we put the canoes in the water and paddled on with renewed vigor.

Shortly after lunch, the terrain and environmental conditions changed dramatically. The river became very narrow and deep with considerable current but no whitewater. The banks became very steep, and rock walls closed in as we entered a small canyon-like area. There was always the subterranean thought about the hidden, unmarked falls that would suddenly seize the canoes and send one hurtling toward a quick ending in the boiling chasm below. There were no hidden falls and no rapids, just good river paddling.

The fatigue of the portages forgotten, we let the beauty of the North Country sink in. The mood and place were ripe for fishing, and all six of us tried our hand. In about two minutes, Gary had a hit and landed a small three-pound laker. Brian and Carl were near the right shore, and Brian eventually had to get onto shore to land a nine-pound laker.

Fred and Chuck had drifted into a wide, shallow eddy, where Chuck tied into a very large fish. As he was working that one, Gary had another hit and landed another fish. The *Harricana VI* and *Wakemaker II* had drifted

Brian and his nine pound lake trout.

downstream about a quarter of a mile when the HMS Victory joined them with a nine and three-quarter-pound great northern pike. As we already had enough fish, we revived and released the northern.

This was the site and the moment "the great controversy" began. Due to the abundance of good size lakers, Carl, the fishing expert of the party, was very glad we threw back the "good-for-nothing" northern pike. According to Carl, these "fish" were terrible and should be eaten only to avoid starvation. In actual fact, Gary preferred lakers to the northern, but in the cold, fast, clear waters there was nothing wrong with the great northern pike. They were not bony if filleted properly and ere excellent eating. For the sake of argument, the rest of the party adopted the reverse position. There was nothing wrong with the northern except for the bad taint in the water brought on by too many lake trout!

The river emptied into Kasmere Lake. The sky was clear, the temperature mild, we had a light wind, and everyone felt good. It had been a long, hard day, and it was getting late (1645). So we made camp at a small, shallow bay on a sandy beach. Camp made, chores completed, we all sat around, sullen and brooding. Everyone was procrastinating; no one wanted to do it, and no one was willing to be first. It had to be done, but the idea was absolutely frightening; in fact, we all rationalized it was probably dangerous and should not be attempted.

Now what, you may ask, could possibly upset this experienced crew to such a degree, particularly in light of the rigors of the past several days and our obvious mastery of this wild country? *A bath, that's what*! Normally on these river trips, a daily dip was the order of things. With water temperatures in the forties and air temperature only a little above, one didn't casually go for a dip; with the exception of Greg, none of us had cleaned up since we'd left Minnesota, and Greg's quick dip was back on June 17.

Greg broke the ice (not really, but almost as the water temperature was 40°F) and plunged in with a Tarzan war cry; submerged; and, within seconds, blasted out with an even louder cry of protest. Gary was next. He stripped down and soaped up but complained that even this part was gruesome. He did not have it in him to dive as Greg had done but strode out into about four feet of water and plunged under. The cold water sent a shock wave through his whole system. A numbing sensation grabbed his whole body, and he came up gasping for air. He was in the water for a total of less than forty-five seconds, but it seemed like an hour.

The other crew members followed suit. And after the ordeal was over, it was the general consensus that it was worth it. We all felt invigorated and ready to take on a grizzly.

After dinner, we all relaxed, caught several fish from shore in two feet of water, and took a long hike up the hill to soak in the environment. The entire day had been full, challenging, and tiring. We'd covered seventeen miles. But with the portages and all, it was sufficient and then some. Everyone slept soundly.

Chapter 8

Kasmere Lake

Day 4: 22 June 1978

The temperature was again cold, 30°F, as we awoke to a beautiful morning. It was very clear, and there was a touch of frost on the landscape. The previous day had been very hard, and we were particularly hungry. Breakfast is not desired by many people, but when canoeing in the North Country everyone looks forward to each meal with relish. Breakfast consisted of eggs, Spam, fresh lake trout, hot chocolate, and coffee. The entire crew began to jell, and breaking camp was much more organized than it had been a few days previous. The total time spent from awakening to getting on the water was about the same, but tasks were quickly put to rest, giving everyone more time to enjoy the moment.

At 0710, all three canoes cut water and headed northeast on Kasmere Lake. The morning was excellent for canoeing, and within a half hour, wool shirts started to come off. Twenty minutes later, Gary took off his cotton flannel, and it isn't long before both Greg and Gary were shirtless. The air temperature was in the high fifties and climbing. There was a slight wind at our back (Murphy must have had it rough the day before as well, as he obviously wasn't up yet), and paddling was pure joy. It was the kind of morning that one would find in an advertisement for experiencing the North Country. We were making about four miles per hour through the southwestern arm of Kasmere Lake. The lake was large, consisting of five large arms or bays, about seven miles long by two miles wide. Our path took us the length of the southwestern arm and completely across the eastern arm to the outlet of the Thlewiaza River.

As we paddled along, everyone commented on the deep blue color of the lake. In the distance, we noticed a thin, pale gray-blue line. There was considerable conjecture as to what it was. Even ice was brought forth as a possibility, but this was rejected. It was far too warm for ice.

We watched the thin gray-blue line for about ten minutes. It did not change in appearance, and we conclude it was a mirage. Attention was diverted to other things for a while and then suddenly brought back to the thin gray-blue line with intense concern. It had taken on form and structure. The gray-blue line was not a mirage; it was pack ice! The southwest wind had blown it to the north end of the lake.

Ten minutes of vigorous paddling brought us to the edge of the pack; we took the water temperature—36°F. Everyone was excited; this was a new adventure not encountered by any of us before. It also brought our forward progress to a halt, as there was ice as far as one could see. Fred and Chuck moved off almost due north following a wide channel in an attempt to find a path through the ice. The *Harricana VI* and *Wakemaker II* hugged the south shore doing the same. Fred and Chuck soon ran out of open water and rejoined us.

We poked along crashing into the ice, using the canoes as icebreakers. The channel was getting narrower, and we could not break the ice for more than two or three feet right near water's edge. Our progress was slowing, and the seriousness of the situation was beginning to sink in. There was a tremendous amount of ice out there, and even with mild temperatures in the 70s and 80s, it would take a week or more to melt. A very strong north-northeast wind might break it up somewhat faster. At this point, there was a gentle southern breeze, and it looked like we were going to get to know Kasmere Lake quite well. No one was worried yet; the excitement and newness of the adventure prevailed, and we were having a lot of fun.

We neared the end of the small channel and discussed our predicament. We were dead in the water; unless some unforeseen stroke of luck was about to descend upon us, we would be late in making Nueltin Lake and may not even get to Eskimo Point. Frankly, there was little concern about

Thlewiaza-Seal Rivers: Challenge of the Ice

either of these consequences; right now, our concern was how, where and when would we get through Kasmere Lake?

Sealand helicopter broke the ice so we could pass.

Just then, we heard a distant syncopated *chop-chop-chop* of a helicopter! Minutes later our friend (using the word with true positive feeling this time) the Sealand Helicopter came into view, and we were all madly waving our paddles. The pilot saw our signal and veered our way. What an incredible break! He circled twice and then pulled away some distance. He landed on the ice about fifty yards out. The ice broke under the chopper weight. He rose, moved over and landed again; and again, the ice broke. It did not look like he was going to land when we realized what he was doing. He was breaking the ice for us on purpose, trying to show us a way through! Stupendous! Incredible! Super!

The pilot landed the helicopter on a small rocky point of land about a hundred yards away. The *Wakemaker II* led a mad hundred-yard dash over to the chopper. A quick consultation followed, and the pilot told us we probably could get through if we moved quickly. The light southerly wind would not hold forever, and opened channels were very small.

View out the left window of the helicopter showing extensive ice.

By invitation, Fred, Brian, and Gary grabbed their maps and piled into the helicopter. Once in the air, they saw several long, narrow open water channels snaking out through the large ice pack. Some of them went on for miles and then dead-ended; a few made it clear through the eastern arm of the lake to the outlet of the Thlewiaza River. The best one was along the south shore of the eastern arm, but the open water was only six to ten feet wide in places. We marked the channels on our maps and made mental note of landmarks and false leads.

The pilot began to climb to give us a view of the entire area. Putahow Lake to the north was totally frozen in. Nahili Lake (the next big lake on our route) was frozen in. And then, on the distant horizon, we saw Nueltin Lake, an immense white sheet. It looked like a glacial ice pack. It was instantly clear that Nueltin Lake, if we made it that far, would be the end of the Thlewiaza River trip for 1978. There was simply no way that ice sheet was going to melt for at least a month.

The only way to scout a rapid 30 feet off the river, down the center at 80 knots.

After the synoptic view of the river and surrounds from several thousand feet, the pilot swooped down over the river and traveled upriver toward Kasmere Lake. He ran about seven miles along the river. It was neat to map the rapids in a chopper at thirty feet. All three of us got a good impression of several rapids and where to run them.

On the way back to the canoes, the pilot also pointed out an old Indian burial ground. We marked the maps and were eager to get back to our waiting bowmen and get underway. The pilot landed; we were genuinely appreciative of his efforts, thanked him, and shoved off.

In spite of the potential seriousness of the situation, the next two hours were fun. The canoes slid through the openings like silent sea monsters. Occasionally we had to break the ice, and the sound of raw aluminum on honeycomb ice broke the silence with sharp tearing noises. The weather held, and we made it to the flowing, clear water of the Thlewiaza River.

After Kasmere Lake, the river picked up very little current, and there was no whitewater. We experienced about an hour of gentle open river paddling, and with the morning drawing to a close, it was time for lunch. A flat, open peninsula at the foot of a very large, long esker was our lunch spot, and we dined on cuisine of bread and soup.

After lunch Greg, Fred, and Gary climbed the esker to see the Indian burial ground. On the way, we found an incredible patch of bearberries, and we gorged ourselves.

The view from the top of the esker was excellent, yet it defied the true nature of the environment, for although we could see for miles around, we saw no ice. Yet we knew from flying over this area only hours before that huge ice sheets covered all the large lakes, effectively blocking passage.

Thlewiaza-Seal Rivers: Challenge of the Ice

We found the Indian burial ground, and the old wooden markers with crosses indicated they were of Christian faith. It was hard to tell how old the burial ground was because it takes many tens of years for wood to decay in the cold North Country.

Our afternoon hike finished, we piled back into the canoes and found the river was picking up speed. Very shortly we approached the first rapids of the day. All canoes ran the rapids with no trouble. A short while later, we came to another rapid—very short, very fast, and very violent. Because of the cold water, Brian and Carl decided to line this one. Greg and Gary looked it over. It was a straight run and fast drop, with rocks on both sides. The center chute was clear of rocks, but there were three-foot-high standing waves. They decided to go for it.

Gary later described running these rapids:

> I was anxious and scared, but the good kind of scared, the kind that motivates one to do his best. As Greg and I approach the rapids, I could not see where we were headed so pull the canoe off dead center (about 10°) to see better. Greg thought I had lost control and tried to correct. I fought his countermovement with a sharp stern rudder. As a consequence, we hit a three and one-half-foot standing wave about three-quarters on. Greg got a good soaking, but we were in no danger of tipping or losing the canoe.

Gary pointed out how important good communication and coordination really is between stern man and bowman. If this had been a rock dodger, we probably would have capsized.

Fred and Chuck followed and went straight through the standing waves with no trouble. Without decking, both of the canoes would have shipped a lot of water, but with the decking, they were dry as a bone.

Late afternoon brought two more rapids that looked too rough to try in the cold water. Consequently, both were lined. This sure beat portaging, even though we got wet up to the waist lining one of them. After the last rapids, the water was deep and fast as it poured into Sucker Lake.

It was getting late in the afternoon, so Brian and Carl took off to look for a place to set up camp, while Fred, Chuck, Greg, and Gary pulled out the rods to catch some fish for dinner. On Gary's first cast he caught a grayling with a large lake trout lure. Although it did not look like grayling water (grayling like fast whitewater), Gary switched to a grayling lure. Greg changed his entire outfit to a lightweight grayling rod and reel. In about two minutes, Greg landed a nice threepound laker.

Gary made a cast into the fastest water he could find and, within a minute, had a hit. He could tell right away that it was not a grayling; it felt more like a nine- or ten-pound laker or northern. The fish did not try to surface, so he figure it for a laker. When he started to reel him in, the fish just took off. Gary had his thumb on the level wind, but the fish took line out so fast he couldn't stop it and burnt his thumb. Wow—some fish! This was no ordinary fish. Gary worked the fish until he thought it was tired and asked Greg to paddle slowly toward shore. Gary knew he was not going to be able to "boat" this fish, as the small grayling lure would pull right out, or the hook would just straighten out.

Then, in about two feet of water, the fish turned around and pulled the canoe back out into deep water. Gary couldn't stop him. Once again, he worked him into shore, but the fish pulled the canoe back out again. Finally, on the third time, Gary said, "Greg, he must be tired. See if you can hoist him in."

Gary worked the fish up to the front of the canoe. Greg grabbed the leader and tried to hoist him into the canoe. As Greg hauled him up out of the water, the hook straightened, and the fish was free. Greg made a lunge and grabbed its tail. Gary was up and out of the canoe in an instant and moved to the bow to help. Greg lost his grip, and for a full fifteen seconds, there was a mad thrashing free-for-all as each of them tried to grab the fish and it tried to get into deeper water. The water was two feet deep, and Gary sat down in the water with his feet against the canoe to trap the fish. The fish tried to swim under Gary, and that was his undoing. Gary grabbed him around the middle with both hands and hung on with all his strength. The fish wiggled free, but by this time Gary had him up and out of the water and plopped the fish into the bow of the canoe. We had him!

Gary was cold but happy! We needed to get Gary a change clothes and near a fire. As it turned out, camp was only thirty minutes away. A fast, invigorating paddle quickly warmed Gary, and he was feeling OK by the time we got to camp at 1745. This was the latest of any day on the trip, but it was worth it; the brute weighed in at sixteen pounds.

Thlewiaza-Seal Rivers: Challenge of the Ice

Gary with his 16 pound lake trout

The day stood out as one of the most memorable, with an incredible diversity of experiences. It began with the idyllic early morning paddle and then the ice pack and helicopter ride, followed by the slow, lazy river paddling and then lunch and our hike to the Indian burial ground. The afternoon saw lots of whitewater and finally the boating (barely) of a sixteen-pound laker. Any one of these would have made it a good day. To have them all in one day was indeed a true treasure.

Chapter 9

Life & Death Struggle

Day 5: 23 June 1978

Gary was overly tired last night and did not sleep well, so Brian had to wake him at 0530. It was cold and dreary. The temperature was 40°F with a brisk wind. After a quick breakfast we were on water at 0640. There was little conversation between anyone as we began paddling. It was probably an emotional overload from the day before; whatever, each of us paddled along in silence as we fought a crisp east wind. It was a time for inner reflection and mediation.

About an hour out, Brian broke the silence. "Look there on the bank; it's a huge animal! It's not moving. Do you see it? Look right there; it's a bear and it looks dead!"

Sure enough, on a sandy point right near the shore was a dead black bear. Instantly, the party came alive, and conversation spewed forth like a pot of boiling water that was too full. What happened? How? When? Well, let's go look. We tied up the canoes; grabbed the cameras; and piled onto shore. The bank was very steep, and getting out of the canoe was tricky. It was a wonder no one dumped in our eagerness to get on shore and explore the situation. The black bear had obviously been in a fight for his life and lost. There was no evidence of man. The only other thing in these woods that had the strength and desire to kill a black bear was a grizzly.

We had been there about ten minutes when Brian reached down and touched the bear. "My God, it's still warm! Let's get out of here!"

Indeed, this was no place to encounter a grizzly. The air temperature was about 45°F, an eight-to-ten-knot wind was blowing, and the wind chill factor must have been near freezing. The incident must have taken place within the last few hours at most. None of us wanted to be scrambling down the steep slope trying to get into the canoes with an angry grizzly on our tail.

We got back in our canoes and were on our way. The black bear and his fate held our attention for some time as we postulated what might have happened. Suddenly, Brian called out, "Look over there on the esker. There he is, a huge grizzly!"

Greg and Gary looked closely, carefully scanning the esker, but could not find him. Fred and Chuck also had trouble spotting the grizzly. The lower part of the esker was covered with dense brush; the middle was patchy; and the top, clear of brush and trees. For several minutes, we all keyed in on Brian and Carl's directions and tried in vain to locate the bear.

Finally, we saw him—a huge, auburn-colored brute. He was halfway down the esker and moving slowly in our direction. He was about two hundred yards away and, even at this distance, conveyed a sense of power and authority. This was his country, and he knew it. It was clear we were intruders, and he was coming over to investigate. He was obviously not too concerned about our presence, but neither was he about to runoff. Gary took two telephoto pictures, one with his 150 mm and one with his 300 mm, when the grizzly was about a hundred yards out.

This was still too far away for good photographs, even with the 30 mm telephoto lens, and Gary nonchalantly suggested we move closer. He was rather strongly overruled by all, with Greg voicing the loudest protest. We backed off to the center of the river to leave plenty of room should the bear decide to charge. The black bear was proof of his prowess, and the crew did not care for an encore.

Of some concern was a rapid immediately downstream. What if we had to portage? Well, it certainly wasn't going to be on the same side of the river as the grizzly, although the river would certainly not stop him if he decided to investigate us, closely. The consensus was that, if we did not irritate him, he would probably go back to his kill. We moved on, ran the rapids, and quickly put several miles between the grizzly and us.

During the afternoon the weather warmed, the skies cleared and it was a super day for paddling. We had not gone very far when we encountered the first rapids of the afternoon. There was fast water, several large rocks and haystacks, but by staying close to the right side everyone made it through with no problem. Running a rapid is paradoxical; on the easy ones the trick is to take the roughest spot you can find to make it more challenging; as the rapids got harder, one gains immense pleasure in reading the water to find the easiest, least dangerous way through. The center of these rapids was a boiling mass of white water and rocks and no one would attempt it, but there was a narrow strip within six feet of the right shore that was relatively calm. We all took pride in "sneaking" through as it were. It was a good omen as we encounter nine more rapids during the afternoon and run all but the last one, which was lined without even getting wet.

Fred and Chuck take on a classic Thlewiaza "rock dodger"

With the grizzly some fifteen miles behind us, there was a marked change in the countryside. We entered a low marsh area with muskeg swamps on both sides. There were no hills or eskers anywhere around. The black spruce was very stunted (about fifteen feet tall), and the river took a slow, twisting meander pattern. The river broke around a large island and we took the left-hand route that was shallow and twisting. The current was moderate. This would be ideal country for moose somewhat later in the season. There was no aquatic vegetation emerging yet, and the moose were still in the winter habitats. In fact, with the exception of the bears, wildlife had been very scarce.

It was about 1500, and we had one more marked rapid just ahead. Brian suggested we run the rapid and make camp at the head of another rapid about a quarter mile downstream. Camp was really stuck in the bushes, yet it served us quite well.

After dinner, the conversation centered on the ice on Nueltin Lake and the ultimate fate of our canoe trip for 1978. Our helicopter ride two days previous confirmed that Nueltin Lake was iced in. Brian was sure we couldn't even make the Southern Cross that we counted on. The choice was clear—call it quits at Nueltin Lake or attempt the escape south to the Seal River. Our failure to get full map coverage of the Seal River back at Lynn Lakes took on its full impact. Brian had studied the Seal River quite extensively and knew that, from the point where our maps stopped to Hudson Bay, there were no large lakes.

We also knew the river made several large twenty-mile north-south loops but generally headed east. Further, several of Brian's canoeing friends had run the river a number of times. We knew that all of the rapids on the main Seal were runnable by experienced canoeists, although there were several who were marginal. Still, without maps it would be a very chancy situation. Then there was Hudson Bay. Again, we knew the general direction to the town of Churchill, but not the specifics. One can get lost on Hudson Bay in bad weather.

Fred and Brian were still discussing strategy when the others called it quits for the day. It was only 1800, and the sun was high. But they were very tired and went to bed.

Chapter 10

Nueltin Lake

Day 6: 24 June 1978

We set the goal for the day to make Nueltin Lake. The goal was only seventeen miles away, but Brian and Gary wanted to reach Nueltin Lake by noon to meet their dad.

The first task of the morning was an interesting challenge. The night before, camp was rather hastily made above a short, fast, churning, but runnable rapids. The canoes had been portaged about thirty yards downstream after unloading them to make camp. There remained only about twenty yards of rapids to run. Under most circumstances, this would hardly be worth a mention. This morning was different. The sun was directly in our eyes, and a bright glare from the water added to the problem. Gary could barely see water, much less interpret the water currents, which is mandatory when navigating a rapid. All three canoes were quickly running the rock-filled rapids where we banged and scratched our way through. The trick was balance. Fortunately, everyone had the skill required, as we all made it without a tip over.

After the rapids, the river opened up into a narrow lake about six miles long. The weather was excellent; it was warm, and we had a tailwind. By the looks of things, it was going to be a good morning. Chuck and Fred decided to put up a sail. Doing this caused them to drop back about four hundred yards, but they caught up to the others with a combination of sail

Fred and Chuck put up the sail

power and paddle power. The wind was too light to be really effective. When Fred and Chuck stopped paddling, the wind was barely sufficient to keep them even with the other two canoes. Greg and Gary hooked their bow rope to their stern, but the drag was too much, so they cut loose, and Fred dropped the sail.

The river narrowed, and the current picked up. Attention was diverted from the ice on Nahili Lake to the river at hand. It was fun paddling but took concentration because rocks there were here and there, a few two-to three-foot standing waves scattered around, and occasional patches of tricky current. The river was about thirty yards wide; although one certainly couldn't call this a rapid, we had to pay attention to the river.

About a quarter mile further, things got more interesting. Gary described how Greg and he made it through the continuation of the rapids:

> I yelled to Greg, "Watch out—rock on the right—hit it left! 11 o'clock, another one on the left—right draw hard!"
> Greg yelled, "Back paddle! Back paddle—boulder dead ahead!"
> I jammed my paddle deep into the water and pushed forward to cut our speed as I looked ahead. The current was taking us directly toward a large boulder with four-foot haystacks on either side. "I got it," I said. "Let's move to the right and try to get into the calmer water ahead."
> "OK, I got ya," Greg countered.
>
> Greg made several hard, deep right draws, while I paddled on the port side with a series of full-on power strokes. The *Wakemaker II* jumped and sailed past the big rock into the calmer water. I looked around to see how the other canoes were doing. Somehow, I thought they were way back. I was surprised to see Fred slightly behind to the right and Brian only a few yards directly behind. Somehow, they took different routes and never got near the big boulder.
>
> Brian and Carl were grinning from ear to ear. "Some fun!" called Carl. Suddenly, the look on Carl's face turned to sheer terror, and Brian yelled, "Ledge, ledge, *dead ahead*!"
>
> I turned and immediately realized the calm water I thought I was in was an illusion. Not more than fifteen yards ahead was a semicircular string of boulders and rocks forming about a two and a half- to three-foot ledge. The chance of hitting a rock was nearly 100 percent. Turning sideways would be disastrous. The canoe would probably fill with water and wrap itself around a rock—end of canoe trip! Greg and I surveyed the situation and decided we had one chance. There was an open chute slightly ahead and well to the left. Someone behind yelled, "Left."
>
> Greg and I were already into action. Reaching as far over as possible and as rapidly as possible, we made a hard draw on the port side. We

gave it all we had. I thought my lightweight Sawyer paddle was going to break. We barely made it. The bow made it into the chute but hit a rock broadside at mid-canoe. Greg and I saw it coming and counterbalanced.

The *Wakemaker II* had enough forward momentum to continue after the crunch, and we were through without a tip over but with a slightly lighter canoe, as it left quite a bit of aluminum on the rock. There was no time to look back to see if the other canoes made it; we were in the middle of a major rapid. There were rocks, standing waves, haystacks, boils, and twisting channels of deeper water crisscrossing all over the place. This was the longest, trickiest rock dodging rapids I had ever been in. The total length was about two and a half miles with literally a dozen of split-second decisions on which way to go, what channel to take, whether to slow down or push ahead hard.

Through it all, no one tipped over or swamped, which was an incredible feat! Some fun! This rapid epitomized the lore surrounding whitewater canoeing. It was the kind one dreams about and the kind that draws one back into the wilderness to try it again. Normally when approaching a rapid, we beached the canoes and thoroughly scouted a rapid before attempting to run it. This was particularly true of long rapids when committing upstream to what looks like an easy path can cause serious problems downstream. This time, the rapid started slowly, and all three canoes were committed without a chance to get out and scout. It built up so slowly over about a mile that, by the time we realized what we were into, it was too late, so we ran it blind.

After the rapids, the river quieted down, and we paddled on for a good half hour, recalling the near misses, the split-second decisions, and the obvious skill and ability of all concerned. It was a truly ego building event.

The river then widened out, increasing the number of channels but also making them shallower and more difficult to navigate. All three canoes took different routes, and we all had to get out of the canoes and drag them the last twenty yards, as the river was about half a mile wide and only a few inches deep. We then found ourselves at Nahili Lake.

Luck was with us; there was a huge ice floe in the north bay and another equally large one in the south bay, while the center of the lake was open. As we proceeded across the lake, we become aware of a strong south wind setting up some good wave action hitting the canoes broadside. To keep the canoe going in a straight line, we had to paddle exclusively on the right side with a threequarter draw stroke. After an hour of this, we became quite tired.

We passed within a quarter mile north of the southern ice pack, and there was a ten to twelve degree drop in the air temperature. The eastern side of Nahili Lake was full of islands, coves, and bays that all looked alike. Finding the outlet of the Thlewiaza River took a while, but we found it. The Thlewiaza gained volume leaving Nahili Lake, and the current was fast. Soon we could hear Nahili Rapids and quickly arrived. The time was 1115 hours, well ahead of schedule.

As we approached, we saw a small, shallow cove on the north side, and tied to the shore were several large rowboats with 25 hp outboard motors. We had obviously found the right place, as the boats were most likely associated with Bill Bennett's Treeline Lodge. There was an easy, open, wellmarked portage (about one-third of a mile) around the rapids. Great! After the portage, we took about an hour to eat lunch and then photographed and explored the rapids. The rapids were long, violent, and dangerous, runnable by experts in a kayak but not by this crew even in our decked canoes. We looked for places where one could sneak through, but there were none. This was one rapid beyond our ability.

Though we could make an ideal camp here, we pushed on to find the lodge. Mr. Gnauck was due to arrive in about an hour, and both Brian and Gary looked forward to the reunion with their dad. We loaded up the canoes and shoved off for another two-mile jaunt to the lodge. There was no ice here, but we knew full well that the lake was frozen in. The open water here was due entirely to the current associated with the river. How far the lake was open, we did not know, but we recalled the Parson Air manager telling us that Treeline Lodge was open to air traffic.

Nueltin Lake: looking north from Treelined Lodge.
The lake had open water for 2 miles and ice for the next 80 miles.

Forty-five minutes of paddling and the help of a stiff south wind brought us to Treeline Lodge. The facilities were situated on top of an esker and consisted of about twelve rustic cabins, a main lodge, a smokehouse, a storage shed, and a crude marina area to meet and service the flights to and from Lynn Lake. The entire operation was supported by well-off or retired businessmen from lower Canada and many US citizens signing on for seven glorious days of fishing.

We looked for Bill Bennett and found him in the main lodge. He was expecting us due to earlier correspondence with Brian. He was a young fellow who, with his wife, had recently taken over the operation of the lodge. They welcomed us and seemed genuinely interested in our journey and how we had fared. Bill told us that only two miles of the lake were open water; everything else was still solid ice, and probably it would be another month before the lake cleared. Even our Southern Cross was iced in. It was clear we would have to end our trip at Nueltin Lake this year or attempt the escape south to the Seal River.

Concerned about lack of maps again weighed heavily on our minds. Chuck asked Bill if he had any maps of the area south that we could buy or borrow. He did not. Then Gary noticed a huge map of the entire Province of Manitoba hanging on the wall. It was a highway map at a scale of 1:1,000,000. This was not exactly what we had in mind; it was not a usable scale or of sufficient accuracy for point-to-point navigation. However, it showed the larger features and did cover all the Seal River and Hudson Bay. Gary made a mental note that it was certainly possible to trace out several copies of this map. Right then, it was time to head down to the water to wait for the arrival of Mr. Gnauck.

The plane was only about ten minutes late. Mr. Gnauck arrived with his friend of some twenty-five years, Frank Perry. They were in good spirits and good health. (Frank was recuperating from a heart attack.)

Mr. Gnauck told us that, as the plane had banked to set down on Nueltin Lake, they'd spotted the green, blue, and red canoes beached about half a mile south of the lodge. They'd figured it was our crew, but neither could believe we'd made it with all the ice.

The entire group met in the two-man cabin assigned to Mr. Gnauck and Frank for a round of drinks and a toast to the future. During the next hour, we recounted our recent adventures, and this led to a rehash of many old hunting, fishing, and canoeing trips.

Late in the afternoon, we all hit Nueltin Lake for some serious fishing. In the *Wakemaker II*, Mr. Gnauck was in the bow, and Gary manned the stern. We fished for two hours, going up to the rapids and back. Mr. Gnauck landed one small laker. No one else in our party landed any fish. Frank had gone out with one of the Indian guides and fared considerably better, picking up five or six lakers in the six-pound category. Earlier, Bill told us the fishermen had been pulling quite a few fish out of these waters, many of them running twenty pounds or more.

The evening brought a relaxed and warm atmosphere. Mr. Gnauck and Frank strolled down to see our campsite and to give us several small lake trout. We had fresh fish for dinner and breakfast. We were all in the story mood again and didn't get to bed until 2200.

We were very fortunate to have had so many safe adventures over the past seven days. Even if we called it quits at Nueltin Lake, the trip would have to be considered a success. No formal consensus had been taken, but the comments indicated that all of us had reached the same conclusion. We were going to escape the ice by going south overland to the Seal River system. After all, now we had a map—albeit a highway map!

Chapter 11

Rest, Then South

Day 7: 25 June 1978

Everyone slept late, as we had the morning off. The only event of consequence was to meet Mr. Gnauck for lunch at a prearranged place on Nueltin Lake, about a mile from camp. It was a warm and sunny day. An excellent morning for taking care of the many repair tasks and chores left undone by the rigors and excitement of the past six days. To start the day off right, Gary took a bath in the shallow water near camp; the water temperature was 48°F. This, coupled with the warm sun and light breeze, made the whole task rather pleasant. Gary even washed his hair and washed one complete set of clothes.

Brian took advantage of the day for relaxing to make biscuits (more affectionately known as "Gnauck's Rocks"). The baking required a special fire. First, we found a large dead log about five inches in diameter. This was cut into four banking logs each about two and a half feet long. Then we cut about two dozen "baking brands." The brands are six to eight inches long and two to four inches in diameter. A normal fire was started and allowed to burn down until there was a bed of coals. Meanwhile, Brian was busy making the batter, a combination of flour and Bisquick. Just as the fire died down, the biscuits were quick browned. The four banking logs were placed around the fire, forming a square. The coals were then cleared from the center and shoved up against the banking logs. The biscuits, in a Dutch oven, were placed in the cleared center area. The baking brands were added periodically at strategic points to maintain an even heat.

A short while later, voila—fresh biscuits! Now the biscuits could be made light and fluffy, but they would quickly fall apart during a typical day. They could also be made rather hard but durable. Knowing the crew would eat almost anything if they were sufficiently hungry, Brian made them on the hard side. Actually, they were reasonably fluffy for the first few days. It was only after a week or so, after they'd lost considerable moisture, that they truly became Gnauck's Rocks. On this particular occasion, Brian made enough biscuits to last two weeks.

Baking complete, Brian, Fred, and Gary strolled to the main lodge to lay out a detailed route for our journey south. Using the highway map as a master, Gary traced off three copies of the last part of the Seal River and the Button Bay area of Hudson Bay. Meanwhile, Fred and Brian laid out a course to take us to the North Seal River. The objective was to balance total distance against the number and difficulty of portages. An average one-third mile portage would take about an hour. This would equate to three or four miles of open lake paddling. A long, hard portage could require a whole morning. After about three hours studying the map, Brian and Fred came up with a reasonable route. The final route would be seventy-five miles and consist of lake paddling, alternating with fourteen portages, most of which would about a quarter mile in length. However, one portage would be about nine miles. A nine-mile portage required twenty-seven miles of walking —two nine-mile trips to carry the canoe, packs, paddles and other gear, plus one nine-mile trip to go back for a second load.

We left the lodge and headed back to camp; the morning was drawing to a close and we were to meet Mr. Gnauck for lunch. Because everything was spread out all over the place, it took a bit more time to clear camp and get underway.

By the time we paddled the mile across the bay, Mr. Gnauck, Frank, and their Indian guide already had lunch prepared. We join them for fresh baked beans and lake trout. Their success at fishing had improved considerably over yesterday afternoon. Between the two of them, they'd boated and released fourteen lake trout, with several in the twentypound category. They were in good spirits and had already taken a liking to the environs of Nueltin Lake.

It came time for goodbyes. Brian and Gary were delighted to visit and fish

Brian, Mr. Gnauck and Gary At Nueltin Lake

with their dad in the wilderness. It was hard for Gary and Brian to say goodbye; part of them wanted to stay on for a few more days of fishing and poking around the backwaters with their dad. Mr. Gnauck was a bit concerned about the forced change of plans, but he was heartened by the fact we had made it this far and obviously knew what we were doing. Final goodbyes made, we piled into the canoes and started the first leg of the "escape south."

Two miles of open paddling in the warm sun brought us to the end of open water and our first portage. A search for a "marked" portage proved fruitless, so we tackled the quarter-mile portage straight on. It was hard, full of dense brush and lots of trees. After the portage, we found ourselves at a small lake, maybe a mile across. We wondered if there were fish in the lake, as there were no connections with the other lakes in the area, but the answer came quickly. A small fourpound laker darted out from under the boat as we started across the lake.

Twenty minutes of paddling brought us to the next portage. We looked it over and knew we were in for a really tough one. We unloaded the canoes but did not immediately pack in. Instead, we scattered to look for the best route through the forest. The portage was short, only a third of a mile long, but it was clearly much more difficult than the previous one. Extremely dense tree growth, very dense brush, fallen logs and boulder fields hampered our progress everywhere. The high ground was not much better. After twenty minutes of looking for a route, we returned to the canoes having reached the same conclusion; we were going to have to bull our way through.

The brush was so dense in places that it was not possible to get through. We backtracked to find a better spot. At times, we just shoved with our legs, forcing a way clear. We were out of breath and sweating profusely when, at last, we saw the blue of Channel Lake.

When Gary finally made it and sat his pack down, he realized that Brian had been there for some time. How we were going to get those seventeen-foot monsters through the tangle was not at all clear. A new problem—no, an old problem, more important than the portage—came to the surface. Ice! Yes, ice on Channel Lake. From where we stood, the lake was frozen in, except for a small strip about ten feet wide along the north shore. The strip was full of navigable honeycomb ice, but it was going the wrong way. Our planned route was due south; the open channel ran due west. Further, we did not know how far it went, but one problem at a time, please; our first job was to get the canoes at least to the lake.

The walk back was relatively easy. Then came forty-five minutes of pushing, shoving, tugging, sweating, and swearing as we literally forced the canoes through the trees and brush. This portage was not nearly as long as the two long portages encountered at Kashmere Falls. Overall, we were in much better shape; no one was exhausted when it was over. But foot for foot, this was the hardest portage we were to encounter on the entire trip, something to look back on.

The portage was mastered, it was now time to tackle the ice. All of us were apprehensive as we proceeded west through the narrow strip of water. It was fun paddling through the ice on a warm afternoon. The sound of ice crunching on aluminum was familiar and no longer had the eerie aura of our first encounter. We paddled west for about two to three miles and then found a rather large open channel heading south. There was no way to tell how far it went, but it was worth a gamble, and it paid off. As we proceed south, the channel widened. Ahead about three miles was a large bald island. It was getting on in the afternoon, so we decided this would be our campsite.

An hour later, we were comfortably settled on the island, which we named Tern Island. The view from the top of the island was spectacular. The deep green of the conifer forest formed a backdrop for the deep blue of Channel Lake, broken by the whitish-blue expanse of the ice pack. We could see that only the north bay was iced in; open water proceeded east of the island, and this would allow us to get back on track in the morning.

Relaxing on Tern Island

Everyone enjoyed relaxing and soaking up the wilderness. Fred, Chuck, Carl, and Greg headed out for some fishing. They paddled to the edge of the ice. We learned that the lakers inhabit the surface water right at the edge. They came back with two lake trout and one northern. Fred, Chuck, Greg, Brian, and Gary were not too sure about dinner. We did not think that one small northern would be enough for all of us; we might have to break down and eat fresh lake trout again.

We had a new treat in store for us before dinner—cocktail hour. And Brian asked if we want them "up" or "on the rocks." We had floating ice chunks for our drinks. As we sat enjoying the day, we became aware of a large concentration of Arctic terns swirling overhead. There must have been thirty or more. The island was apparently a breeding ground and nesting site. The birds were carrying on a courtship display, where one would chase the other straight up until they were out of sight. They would then go into a power dive straight down to make a U-turn within three to five feet of the ground before heading up again to repeat the maneuver.

Dinner was exceptionally good, and afterward, everyone did his own thing. Greg read a book, Fred sewed up his trousers, Chuck and Carl went fishing, and Brian and Gary explored the island. The area abounded with bearberries, a nice after-dinner treat. Gary heard Chuck and Carl get into some good fishing and decided to join them in the *Wakemaker II*. Gary paddled over to the west side of the island and saw a swirl just ahead in about two feet of water. Gary made a cast and *wham*! A small three-pound laker hit. Gary worked it up to the canoe and released it. The second cast was in a little deeper water, and another laker hit. This one, too, Gary brought to the canoe and released. The third cast was toward shore in only a foot of water and another laker hit. Three casts and three fish; it was almost boring. Chuck and Carl also had their share of action. Between them, they had caught and released six lakers. Getting tired of the little ones, Gary put on a very large spoon and headed to deep water. He fished for another forty-five minutes and never had another strike.

It had been a good day, and it was time to turn in. It was hot (65°F), and everyone decided to sleep outside rather than in the tent. We'd started at noon today and covered only seven miles. Everyone knew this was our last easy day; we had a lot of water to cover, and time was running out.

Chapter 12

29 Mile Day

Day 8: 26 June 1978

At 0430, up and out of the sack. Gary had the fire going and was working on his second cup of coffee when Brian joined him. We had a big day planned and wanted to break camp early. There was only one portage planned and no whitewater. Paddling would be confined entirely to Channel Lake. This would consist of weaving in and out of bays, between islands, past coves, and around points to our sole portage some twenty-nine miles away.

This morning was clear, calm, and incredibly beautiful. The first few hours were pure pleasure, warm sunny skies, and no wind. Navigation was tricky at times, as all of the islands encountered did not show up on the map. We made one navigation error that cost us only about two hundred yards. Then at 0900, a wind came up, hitting us three-quarters straight on. As the wind became stronger, the skies clouded up, and we could tell the rest of the day would not be nice.

Stroke, stroke, stroke, pull, pull, pull—the miles passed and paddling became very routine, almost unconscious. We paddled for five and a half hours straight, mostly into the wind. Brian kidded that he had planned it that way: ""Part of our training program in preparation for Hudson Bay," he said.

We were glad when noon came, and we finally stopped for lunch. The refueling break was a welcomed relief.

The afternoon was a repeat of the morning, except the wind increased, and there were scattered showers. Shortly after lunch, we reached the limit of Gary's map, and he had to trust Fred and Brian for navigation. The miles passed, the islands passed, the bays and coves passed, and we paddled on. Then at 1510, we reached the last bay; the day was at an end. Considering the headwinds and all, we had done well, and all felt good about making the goal.

As we pulled into shore, a small thundershower broke, and there was a mad scramble to get the tarp up and gather enough wood for a fire. This task was very easy, as the entire area had been burned off some time ago, and there was much downed and dead wood. The black spruce overstory was dead, and the brush severely set back. As Brian started dinner, Gary looked at Carl, and he knew what that meant. There was a break in the rain, and we hopped into a canoe to catch fish for dinner. Carl landed a small laker within the first few minutes. We fished for another thirty-five minutes and headed back when it started to rain again. As they approached the shore, Gary took a final cast in eight inches of water next to some weeds. A three-pound northern was there to meet the cast. Saved again from eating fresh lake trout!

A new problem was encountered during and immediately after dinner—one we weren't sure we could handle at first—mosquitoes. The warm wind and rain had brought them out. This, in turn, brought out the Cutters, but Carl and Fred had fun in a mosquito-killing contest. Gary thought the winner tallied around a hundred when they quit. It was the first encounter with the little critter and really rather fun.

After dinner, we portaged across an open strip of land half a mile to a new unnamed lake. Because the fire had cleared the brush, it was very easy. When Gary got to the other side, he immediately sat down his pack and made two casts into the new lake. The second cast produced a nice three-pound northern for breakfast. The tent sites for the evening were outstanding; each was placed on a bed of sphagnum moss about two feet deep, wilderness camping at its best.

The sun came out for a bit, and Gary took advantage of it by taking a bath and washing some clothes. He felt invigorated, and it had an added benefit of attracting fewer mosquitoes. It was early, but all were feeling tired so decided to turn in.

It had not been an exciting day; there were no difficult portages, no whitewater, the weather went from good to poor but not bad, and the paddling was hard but not draining. All told, the day was uneventful, yet good. This, too, was part of the wilderness experience.

Chapter 13

Surprises

Day 9: 27 June 1978

    At 0345, Gary woke with a start. He could not remember if his map case had made the portage. The last time Gary recalled having it was noon yesterday. Gary had run out of map coverage shortly after lunch and had put the map case under the decking in the canoe. Gary did not want to lose it, as it contained notes and records from the first part of the trip and his copy of the hand-drawn map of the Seal River. Fortunately, a quick five-minute search turned it up, but by now, Gary was too wide awake to go back to sleep. It was cold (about 44°F), with a sharp north wind blowing. Gary got a hot fire going. Brian joined him a little later, and they had a good morning talking and sipping hot chocolate. It had been many years in the embryonic stage, but the wilderness canoe trip was finally a reality. It was all Gary expected and then some.

    They got the rest of the crew up at 0510, hoping to get an early start. There were at least five, maybe six portages on the route this day. If the portages of the past two days were typical, we would need all the time we could get. The target for today was to get through Booth Lake.

    Everything was tied down in portage configuration; we set off, and a short paddle brought us to the first portage. It was short, three hundred yards on nice open ground, and we made it in record time. Ten minutes of paddling brought us to the second portage. This one had a very small stream associated with it. The stream was only two to three feet wide, just wide enough to float a canoe. Greg and Gary were in the lead, edging along. The stream turned out to be too shallow to float a canoe and, very shortly, ground out on the rocks. As we stepped out of the canoe, it floated, so we line it through to the end. The others followed suit. Everyone got wet, but it sure beat portaging.

Twenty-five minutes of vigorous paddling across a small lake brought us to the next portage. We could not tell from the map exactly what we were up against. It was either going to be several long portages with a few short paddles in between or one "humungous" nine-miler. As we approached, we again encountered a small stream. By carefully picking our way around the rocks and downed branches, we were able to get quite far along before finally grounding out. The resulting portage was only about a quarter of a mile of moderate difficulty, and we arrived at a small five-acre pond.

A very short paddle brought us to the other end of the pond. A stream leaving the pond was not navigable, and we could not line the canoes. We did not attempt a portage either. We slide the canoes! The entire area was covered with two to three feet of ice and snow which had a slight downward slope. One man grabbed the bow rope and pulled, while another kept the canoe from running into the one pulling. We literally slid the canoes to the next lake about three hundred yards away. It was the most incredible method of moving six hundred pounds of men and gear overland that we had ever experienced. All of us took photographs of the process, since no one would believe it unless it was documented.

Chuck pulling a canoe across the snow: The only way to portage

Another twenty-five minutes of paddling, and we arrived at the next portage. This one, too, had a stream associated with it; it was too tricky and rocky to run yet it was definitely possible to line.

Another short paddle brought us to what we thought would be our last portage. The stream was still with us, and it had gained a bit more water, which had nice rapids, fast current, rocks, and channels twisting every which way. In many ways, small rapids were more of a test of canoeing skills than large and dangerous rapids. Further, if one made a mistake it was usually not serious, just embarrassing. We looked it over and felt it was our kind of rapids, so we ran it. Quick reflexes and maneuverability were the name of the game. All three canoes made it through with no problem.

A pattern was developing that we dared not hope would last, but it did. The next "portage" was a rock-dodging, five- to eight-foot-wide stream through a rock garden. We tackled it with gusto. This was what the trip was all about, and we couldn't believe our good fortune. Toward the end of the rapids, the *Harricana VI* got hung up on a rock; Brian and Carl could not break it loose, no matter what they tried. Finally, in desperation, Brian stepped out of the canoe to free it up. He stepped into a four-foot hole and got wet to his waist. With that, we decided it was time for Brian to dry out so landed for lunch.

This ended, in very grand fashion, what could have been a nine-mile portage when Brian and Fred picked a route while at Nueltin Lake four days before. Instead of a long portage, we encountered several small streams where we could line our canoes, a field of ice and snow where we could easily pull our canoes across, ponds that we were able to paddle across, and a navigable stream that was fun to run but was a test of our canoeing skills. We were fortunate because none of this would be possible any other time of the year.

Everyone was in the mood for a warming fire and some hot soup. A more spirited crew would be hard to find. We had prepared ourselves for a long, hard portage and, instead, found good conditions for travel, a tripper's dream come true. After lunch, we christened our little stream the "Booth River" and studied the map very carefully to see what lay ahead. We arrived at Booth Lake, and it looked like our fun was over. It would take about an hour's paddling to traverse Booth Lake and then another stream to take us east. As best we could tell, we would be going against the current. Even if the "portages" were runnable rapids, we would be going the wrong way. Yet, we could not be sure of the drainage. In this part of Canada, a difference in elevation of only a few feet often governs the drainage pattern for many tens of thousands of square miles. The 1:250,000 scale maps did not have the accuracy to portray these small elevation differences. The drainage could possibly be with us, but it did not look promising.

The weather was improving; the wind had died down, and the clouds were beginning to break up. Our wool shirts came off as we hit the open water of Booth Lake. We found the bay and turned left. As we proceeded, everyone was on pins and needles wondering about the current. We were all watching intensely for the first sign of current, a slight riffle, a floating leaf, or a submerged weed. There was no sign. Then, suddenly, we had current, and it was with us—incredible! What's more, there was a rapid to run. The river had grown considerably, and the roar of whitewater told us we had better check it out. A short stop revealed it to be a churning, straight drop with rocks and boulders. The water temperature was still on the cold side, but our confidence had grown over the past nine days, and we thought we could run it.

There had been a few similar rapids back on the Thlewiaza River that we'd lined, but today, there was no stopping this party. We ran the rapid one canoe at a time, with the other two crews standing by in case of a tip over. There were none, and we all gained another notch on our paddles. The afternoon brought still another rapid and another notch on our paddles, as we successfully ran it. The last rapid was exceptionally inspiring, and since it was now 1500, Brian decided to look for a place to camp. In the distance about two miles away, we saw a thin brown line—a sandy beach. What a day!

Tents pitched, wood gathered, and fire started, Carl and Gary volunteer to get some fish for dinner. Being somewhat nonchalant, we figured we could get what we needed in the shallow, sandy cove near camp. Brian gave them only forty-five minutes. Thirty minutes of poking holes in the water proved us wrong. Finally, Carl turned to Gary and said, "This is ridiculous. How long will it take to paddle back to the last rapids?" "Well, with no gear; no wind; and, if we each dig in, maybe twelve minutes," Gary replied.

With that, they hightailed it back to the rapids. Three casts produced three lakers. Carl got two, with the largest running about seven pounds; Gary got one, about four pounds. Carl was exceptionally pleased there were no northern to eat tonight. We did have a special treat in store when we got back—hors d'oeuvres of popcorn and sardines, scrumptious.

After dinner, Fred, Chuck, Carl, and Gary went back to the rapids for some sport fishing. Carl caught four northern and one lake trout. Gary landed three northern, and Fred and Chuck got a northern apiece. All fish were released unharmed. The entire episode occurred in an area of about two acres and in less than an hour's time.

We marveled at what the day had brought. We'd made twenty-two miles, run six rapids, lined two rapids, slid over one, and had two easy portages. All that, and it was great fun!

Carl & Gary with dinner

Chapter 14

North Seal River

Day 10: 28 June 1978

It was quite late, 0515, when Gary finally crawled out of the tent and looked the world in the eye. The day greeted us with a 29°F temperature and a dense fog that covered the countryside. It was a slow morning for everyone, and breakfast was exceptionally good. It was not until 0700 that the fog began to lift, and we finally got on the water at 0725. The morning was clear with no wind. We were on a large unnamed lake, and it was mirror smooth. Brian was concerned about our progress. To make Hudson Bay with a three-day safety margin, we'd have to average twenty-six miles per day. Our late start did not help, and Brian did not like the lack of wind. He felt that there was a tendency for one to slack off just a bit on a totally calm day, whereas, with a slight wind, one gives that little extra effort. Knowing this, Brian was urging everyone on to make time. This we did. If fact, the HMS *Victory* and the *Wakemaker II* pulled into a nice sandy beach for lunch a good third of a mile ahead of the *Harricana VI*. A check of Fred's map revealed we had made fifteen miles. This bit of news brightened our spirits and put us in the proper frame of mind for the afternoon.

Shortly after lunch, we reached a major milestone—the North Seal River. This river was different. Four days ago, we'd left the Thlewiaza River as a young, vigorous, and growing river but one that was far from mature. Ice forced us overland where we found and christened the Booth River. The Booth took us from its birth to its death until it finally drowned in the unnamed lake of the morning's paddle.

We were now in the current of the North Seal River, and we were aware of its immense power and strength. We joined it many miles from the headwaters, and it was quite different from anything some of us had canoed before. Most of the previous whitewater experience had been on rivers the size of the Booth and Thlewiaza Rivers. The North

Seal River was not the type of river one took command of. Rather, if you knew what you were doing, it let you come along for the ride.

About two miles downstream, we encountered our first rapids. Very different—immense, powerful, strong current and four-foot-high standing waves. There were rocks, but not like we'd encountered before; here, the problem was one of reading the current and not getting sucked into a haystack, a boil, or a big standing wave that could not be handled. Because of the strong current, midcourse corrections were very difficult, if not impossible. One could change directions, but it had to be planned out and executed well ahead of the trouble spot.

Everyone got through the first rapids and moved on downstream. Sometime later, we encountered a second rapids. We had loads of fun riding out the four- and five-foot waves. It was much like riding a bronco. Despite the churning water, it was not a difficult run, and all made it with ease.

Neither of the first two rapids was marked on the map. Now, we finally came to the first marked rapids. This was a rapid of a different vintage altogether. It was not as long or as rock invested as the Nahili Rapids, and at first, we didn't think it was as dangerous. The volume of water, however, was considerably greater, and it made a distinct "portage" impression on everyone. It was getting on in the afternoon, so we decided to make camp on top of a wooded esker at the head of the rapids. The canoes were portaged about three hundred yards around the rapids for an easy start in the morning.

When Gary got back to camp after the portage of the canoes, he realized that he was not feeling up to par. He was listless and uncomfortable. Making camp and getting the fire started was a real chore. Gary become aware of several very large blisters full of clear fluid forming on his hands. Greg came down with something similar. The blisters were not due to rubbing or abrasion but some kind of infection. Neither Greg nor Gary was all that concerned, but they started to take antibiotics anyway. The wilderness of Northern Canada was not the place to come down with an illness.

Fred kept our string of successful fishing days alive by catching a northern just above the rapids. Gary tried his hand at grayling fishing for about fifteen minutes. He had several strikes but didn't land any.

Although the day was still young, Gary's hands felt hot with a burning sensation, so he decided to turn in.

Gary did not know it then, but his hand infection would get worse throughout the trip and became a major element in the days ahead.

Chapter 15

Lost Gear

Day 11: 29 June 1978

    The crew was on the water at 0710. The first ten miles were absolutely outstanding. We put in just below the rapids and immediately experienced very fast water. We tried to maintain a reasonably close distance between canoes, but the current was strong, approaching ten miles per hour, and we became separated on several occasions. The two lead canoes (Greg and Gary were last) saw a moose, one of the very few we were to encounter on the entire trip.

    We came to the first major rapids of the day without warning. The river did not form the typical calm area just prior to the rapid. The North Seal was in high water and just poured ahead. The rapid looked rough, with two large rocks at the bottom. The current was very fast and did not allow us to get to shore to scout. To gain a better view, all three stern men momentarily stood up, a practice that would continue throughout the Seal River. Not having that many options, we went for it down the center chute. There were large (four- to five-foot) standing waves dead center, and we took the brunt of them straight on. The turbulent current patterns swung the canoes around, and it took concentration and hard paddling to maintain balance and a straight course. All told, it was a super run—no mishaps, and all commented on the value of the decking.

    We were moving so rapidly with the swollen river and were so busy watching the river that we lost track of our position on the map. This, coupled with a map compilation error (the only one found), led to a short three-hundred-yard portage. We encountered a large (several hundred acre) island, and the map showed a larger channel to the right. The map was wrong; the channel on the right stopped in a dead-end bay, with only a very small trickle of water proceeding forward.

    The portage was easy. When we loaded up the canoe to shove off, Gary discovered he had lost his ditty bag containing his Gore-Tex rain gear. The entire crew pitched in and spent an hour looking for it. It was gone, damn, damn, damn! Gary was very upset and emotionally depressed. It put a damper on the entire morning. Fortunately, Carl had brought along an extra waterproof poncho. It would do in case of rain, but the thought of losing his rain gear was maddening. Gary had either lost it on the portage, when he'd taken a spill, or it had never got aboard first thing out in the morning. Greg and Gary had an oral checklist they went through every time they loaded up the canoe to avoid this from happening; whatever, it was gone, and Gary had best forget it.

We moved on. Gary did not eat much for lunch, still brooding about his lost gear. The afternoon brought more whitewater. The fun and excitement of taking on four-foot waves snapped Gary out of his low.

Chapter 16

News of a Friend

Day 12: 30 June 1978

At 0345, Gary was up and functioning. An early start was needed, and our paddles began to cut water at 0600. The goal today was to make thirty miles and camp somewhere on Stoney Lake. Our most productive paddling was in the morning. After lunch, there was one more two- to threehour shot at attaining the goal, but if we hadn't done well by noon, we would probably not make the goal.

A strong headwind greeted us during the morning, but the crew was well broken in and tore into the wind and waves with strong determination. The wind presented a challenge that was met and beaten. Greg and Gary had the strokes down pat, almost unconscious. The canoe was lighter, and they could really move the "machine" along at a good clip. The wind held throughout the morning, but by 1100, we picked up a very fast river current and, by noon, had clocked twentythree miles! What's more, no one was overly tired.

The afternoon brought more strong winds, and when we finally reached Stoney Lake, our progress slowed a bit. The open expanse of the lake tossed up some pretty good waves.

"It's all in training for the Bay," Brian called out.

There was a long pull across an open bay to the protected lee shore. We made the shoreline at around 1400 and found an abandoned Indian campsite. This called for a break and a little exploration. The camp had recently been used, but no one was around. There were several small tents used as individual sleeping quarters and one large tent. The large tent contained some food, including canned goods, beer, fishing gear, and a single-shot 12-gauge shotgun. Brian said there was a major Indian settlement about three days south of here on Tadoule Lake. This was probably an outpost used for trout fishing (netting). The general vibes were not good, so we decided to move on.

Two miles further, we found a beautiful sandy beach in a protected cove. It was only 1445, but we had exceeded our goal, as we were at mile thirty-two and would not likely find as nice a campsite as this for the rest of the trip. The day was very warm, so everyone took a bath, followed by a short swim. No one took the water temperature, but it must have been in the high fifties or low sixties in the shallows near shore.

Afterward, we lay on the beach and enjoyed sunbathing. We had a very long cocktail hour, and Brian baked some sweet bannock. Bannock was a particularly good treat, and we all asked him to do it again before the trip was over. As dinner was being prepared, Fred decided to try for some fish. He walked to a point of land near camp and gave about fifteen casts with no luck. He fell out of the fishing mood as quickly as he'd gotten into it, and no one else, not even Carl, picked up the challenge. This was the first day since the start of our trip that we didn't have fresh fish with the meal.

Gary's hands really swelled up in the hot afternoon sun. The blisters covered his fingers and the back of his hands. There was a clear, pussy drainage from the open ones. Breaking them open did not dry them out. A second blister quickly formed under the new skin surface. Gary found wearing gloves helped protect them from the sun and also from the early morning cold. No one knew the cause or why only Greg and Gary had blisters; however, Brian said that, on the previous trip, the "wood men" had also gotten the blisters. Maybe it was some fungus in the wood.

Brian and Gary turned in early. The rest were in the sack by 2200. Then about 2300 (it was still light at this time), several Indians came to the main tent and talked with Fred and Carl. We learned from the Indians something that kept our attention for the next several days. Some background was necessary to understand the significance.

A good friend of Brian and Greg, Glen Sorensen, was traveling in these waters with his own party. Brian had introduced Glen to wilderness canoeing. Fred had also gone on a trip with the two of them. Glen had been planning his own trips for the past several years. According to Brian, Glen had a party of eight (four canoes). This was the first time two of the crew had been canoeing. They had a sixty-day trip planned that started in Southern Indian Lake (several hundred miles southeast of our present location) about a week before we started our trip. Glen was to work his way north to the main Seal River, go upstream on the Wolverine River, and work his way north via portaging through lakes and small streams until he reached the Thlewiaza River. In fact, Brian and Glen had arranged to leave a message at a major rapid. It was expected that Brian would make the point first. Glen, of course, did not know of our change in plans, and he also was probably not aware he was heading into the severe obstacle of the ice.

We learned from the Indians that Glen and had been crew were at Tadoule Lake three days before. The best that Glen and his crew could be doing was fifteen to eighteen miles a day, but Brian figured it was closer to twelve to fifteen miles a day. Using fifteen as an average, Glen would be within forty miles of our present location. There was an outside chance we could catch him before he turned north on the Wolverine.

The day went fast. We ran three rapids, though none were exceptionally noteworthy. We had wind most of the day, but that did not significantly slow our progress. It was a good day.

Chapter 17

Stoney Lake

Day 13: 1 July 1978

We broke camp and were on the water at 0605. Stoney Lake was about three miles wide by twenty miles long. The morning was clear with a bright sun, perfect temperature, and absolutely no wind. On this particular morning, the entire lake was absolutely mirror-smooth. Sitting in the canoe at about three feet off the water, one could see about five miles to the horizon. In the entire field of view, there was not a riffle or wave. It was very rare to see such a large body of water this absolutely motionless, mirror-like.

The canoes sliced the surface and set up eddies and waves that trailed out behind the canoes for a hundred yards. We paddled the entire length of the lake. Silence dominated the scene. We paddled well away from shore and heard no sound except the paddles dipping the water and the sound of the Grumman canoes as they slice through the calm water. At one point around 0900, the three canoes were in an almost perfect equilateral triangle about a mile apart. Gary could not believe what he was experiencing; it was so unreal. He felt he was participating in a Walt Disney fantasy, expecting Tinker bell to suddenly appear on the water and lead us to Peter Pan.

At 1030, our party reached the end of Stoney Lake and encountered the first ripples on the surface of the water—the current of the North Seal River. Downstream, a short distance was a major rapid. The river was large, the current and power truly impressive. All three stern men stood to read the rapids. Since hitting the North Seal, Gary deferred to Brian and Fred the honor of being first down the rapid. They both had more experience in running big river rapids than he had, and he felt no compunction whatsoever about following. Brian spotted a channel just ahead to the left, and we all scrambled to position our canoes properly. Unlike many earlier rapids, midcourse corrections were nearly impossible.

Positioning accomplished, we dug in and, within seconds, were experiencing four-to six-foot standing waves. Greg was hit full on as several waves broke over the bow and two large waves hit at mid-canoe, drenching Gary. The power draw, back paddle, and bracing strokes were critical to maintain balance. Excitement and tension ran high as we worked our way through the rapid. Everyone made it without mishap. A short while later, we encountered another set of rapids of the same ilk and breeding, and these too were successfully run.

The third rapids of the day were something else again. As we approached, we could tell the rapid was long, big, and ferocious. The roar of the water was loud, and the churning whitewater awesome. Yet, it did not seem dangerous, and we decided to run it.

It began much like the previous rapids; Greg and Gary were yelling, screaming, and having a ball. The high water had eliminated most of the rocks, and the main concern was balance and position. Gary looked ahead and caught a glimpse of Brian and Fred fighting desperately for space off to the right. Gary did not understand why they were madly drawing right. The waves we experienced were running five feet but manageable, and there were few rocks. Then suddenly Gary realized the current had pulled his canoe too far left, and ahead were huge, eight- to ten-foot standing waves and haystacks. Greg yelled something, but Gary could not understand above the roar of the water. All Gary knew was we had to get out of here fast!

Gary paddled hard on the right side with strong draw strokes and Greg did likewise. Unlike many earlier rapids, where Greg and Gary could whip the Wakemaker II around at will, their paddling was having almost no effect. The current was pulling them closer to the big waves. Gary's thoughts were blurred, and he lost his sense of position as fear overran logic. Finally, their paddling fortunately did have an effect, and they just edged out to the right of the big waves. It was a long rapid, and we had to keep at it the whole time.

Afterwards, there were greetings and salutations from all canoes. This was the largest set of rapids we had encountered and run to date, and it was a good feeling to say we'd made it. Greg and Gary shook hands on this one. Another in a long line of ego builders.

Ahead was Shethanie Lake. There would be no more whitewater for the day, and we were in one of the best fishing sites of the entire trip—deep water, fast current, many eddies and crosscurrents, as well as shallow, quite backwaters. We fished for about half an hour. Fred landed a nice eight-pound trout, while Carl picked up two, and Gary got one.

The river dumped into Shethanie Lake, the last big lake of the trip, and the place where the South Seal and North Seal merge. Fred and Carl wanted to stop early; Brian wanted to push on awhile. As this was our last chance to try for big lunkers, Brian relented, and we made camp at 1500 on a neat rocky point of land.

Brian put out an extraordinary dinner, and with the fresh lake trout, our plates were stacked high. The amount of food we consumed was amazing. We were eating over twice as much as normal yet had not gained or lost weight. The daily intake was well matched by our output.

Brian kept the food delicious & plentiful.

After dinner, Gary spent some time taking close-up photographs of the flowers, lichen, and berries. A little later, Greg joined Gary for a walk. The environment was changing. They were still in the taiga but with a transition into tundra. There were patches of twenty to thirty acres free of trees. They walked along the edge of one of these patches and found several shorebirds in bright breeding plumage. Off to their left was a large swamp with stunted black spruce five to ten feet high. Beyond was high ground where the spruces reached thirty to fifty feet in height. The walk lasted about an hour and took them through the swamp and into the larger trees and then back to camp in a wide circle. The trek was uneventful, except that, in the swamp, they awoke hordes of mosquitoes who followed them back to camp.

A light breeze had come up, and fortunately, it blew the mosquitoes away, so again we were saved from the curse of the North Country.

Fred and Carl went out for lunker lakers and were quite successful. Fred caught a twelve-pounder and Carl a fifteen-pounder.

This was another outstanding day. Beginning with the incredible mirror calm of Stoney Lake, then exciting, demanding whitewater and ending with an early camp and time to explore and relax. Yet, we only made twentyeight miles. We will never make it to Hudson Bay on schedule at this rate. Tomorrow we will tackle Shethanie Lake, our last big lake. Then it will be all North Seal River. Perhaps we will be able to make up the difference with a full day of river paddling if we don't have to portage.

Chapter 18

Shethanie Lake

Day 14: 2 July 1978

A fierce wind woke us at 0300. A major low-pressure system had moved in, and the nice weather of the past two weeks was gone. It was cold and raining lightly, with an eleven-knot wind blowing from the east. The goal today was to make at least thirty miles, eighteen of them on Shethanie Lake directly into the wind.

Gary got a roaring fire going at 0500 and rousted everyone awake. Brian prepared a huge six-pancake breakfast, plus a large hunk of lake trout for each person. Numerous cups of hot chocolate were consumed, as we knew it was going to be a hard, cold day.

Camp was cleared and we tackled the winds on Shethanie Lake. The wind was cold, and the accompanying rain was miserable as it stung our faces. This was by far the hardest paddling we had experienced. The shoreline crept by slowly even with enormous energy output. Although Grumman canoes had incredible durability and load carrying capacity, they were not the canoes for high winds. They rode high in the water with a lot of freeboard. Fighting a wind was tough.

Only Brian had a map now, and that was with a small scale. Many of the smaller islands did not show on his map, and navigation became more uncertain. Brian selected a crisscross pattern through the length of Shethanie, trying to take advantage of the lee shores and protection of the

Shethanie Lake; a change in the weather

many islands that dotted the lake. We crossed directly over to the opposite shore, going out of our way to gain the advantage of the lee shore. It was a very hard pull, and the benefit was short-lived, as we quickly came to the end of the peninsula and had to turn into the wind. The intermittent rain slowly began to have an effect, and everything got wet.

Lunchtime arrived, and we dove into hot soup and delicious Gnauck's rocks covered with jam, swigging them down with hot chocolate. The morning behind us, we were all reluctant to tackle the afternoon paddle. We had three-quarters of Shethanie Lake beaten. Another six miles of lake, and then we should find the outlet of the mighty Seal River. At Shethanie Lake, the North and South Seal Rivers merged, forming one of the major wilderness rivers in this part of Canada. The only bright spot was the possibility of catching Glen and his party. Brian did not believe Glen would move out on a day like this, particularly with an inexperienced crew. Lunch was over, and the fire was going out, so we hurried to get back into the canoes and continued paddling. There is nothing worse than standing around in the rain watching a fire go out.

The storm did not let up throughout the afternoon. We continued to battle the wind and the rain and at one point we lost track of our location. We knew somewhere ahead within two-miles was the outlet of the Seal River. There were many islands and coves that did not show up on Brian's map and we did not want to waste several hours looking for the outlet of the river. Just as we began to question if we were in the right place, we encountered current and soon found ourselves on the Seal River. Brian did a truly impressive job of navigating. The river was a huge, massive, rolling, volume of water heading on its one-way journey to oblivion. Unfortunately, the countryside was very low and flat which offered no protection from the wind. At one point, we had a strong current pulling us downstream and strong winds pushing us back upstream. If we stopped paddling the wind would win. We made camp at the confluence of the Wolverine and Seal rivers. The campsite was in a dense stand of spruce well back from the river. Greg and Carl took the canoes over to the other side of the Wolverine and upon their return they reported signs of fresh tracks and portage marks (there was a rapid immediately upstream on the Wolverine). We missed Glen by a few hours.

Inside the shelter of the trees, it was rather nice and the fury of the wind was gone. Greg and Gary took a walk and chanced upon a spruce grouse. These birds were very tame and this one looked like it could make our day by becoming dinner. We got within fifteen feet and took careful aim with a rock, but missed. Well, there was always fish to catch, but with the weather as miserable as it was no one volunteered and we had another night with no fish for dinner. (After dinner, Greg and Carl did catch a very small northern which they threw back.)

The tent and sleeping bag felt good. This day had been by far the hardest. Gary had commented at dinner that if someone made him do this, he would consider it cruel and unusual punishment. This was a good summary of the day. Yet, there was something satisfying about taking on the North Country during a "big blow."

Chapter 19

Cold! Wind! Fog! Drizzle!

Day 15: 3 July 1978

The storm had not let up as we got up this morning. It was another six-pancake breakfast, and we needed them to face the day. The air temperature was 38°F, and the water temperature was in the low fifties. A dense fog swirled over the water surface to meet fine, misty drizzle driven by a strong easterly wind. Our course would take us directly in the wind, and it was expected to be much colder than yesterday. We dressed warmly, with all available clothing.

We were on the water at 0730, and in a very short distance, we heard our first rapids. Fred and Chuck were in front to the right, Brian and Carl a little farther ahead to the left, and Gary and Greg in the middle. The wind was blowing the fine mist directly at us. The water was dark purple-black, with flecks of gray at the wave tops. The sky was a uniform gray and the white, swirling fog rose up from the water surface to meet the sky, masking all but the fifteen yards immediately in front of the canoes. We could not see the rapids, but we could hear them. Gary desperately wanted to capture this scene with his camera, but the demands of the river and the fear of the rapids were too much; Gary didn't dare risk it.

It turned cold again

The three canoes cautiously approached our unseen foe. It seemed as if we were about to be swallowed by the roaring, dark purple menace. Then the purple of the river changed into an eerie, violet-gray boiling mass of water as we entered the rapids. No one spoke; we just back-paddled slowly, braced, and edged the canoes along in the fog-shrouded whitewater. The waves got larger, and black rocks emerged from behind the white mask of the fog to block our way. We looked ahead, straining to get a better idea of where we were and where we were going. There was nothing but violent purple water giving birth to white swirling fog, which rose to merge with the gray waterinfested sky.

Gary kept Fred's and Brian's canoes in sight, hoping to avoid a disaster if either of them encountered one and thought, *My God, where are we going? Where does this lead?*

Then it was gone! The roar of the black-purple monster was behind us. The waves smoothed out; the river quieted but retained its dark, foreboding aura; and the fog continued to slow our progress.

A short while later a second rapids announced its presence with a dull, ominous roar. The Seal River was truly huge; We could not see its total extent, but could hear rushing water way off to the left and to a considerable distance to the right. We were three tiny specks somewhere out in the middle. We knew all the rapids on the lower Seal were runnable, but there were some large, dangerous rapids that need to be scouted. None of them should be taken blind. Gary wondered, did Fred and Brian know this?

No one was comfortable with the present situation, yet we all proceeded nonetheless. The second rapids were mastered and then a third. We were doing all right, except the elements were beginning to take their toll. It was very cold, and our hands were cold and stiff. During the rapids, we all forgot the cold, the wind, and the rain. In between, that was all we could think about. The cold drove its presence deep into our bones, and shivers were common.

By noon, the fog had lifted. We could now see the extent of the Seal River and gain some idea of what we were dealing with. We quickly found a place to have lunch and built two fires. One was a huge bonfire for warmth, the other a smaller one for cooking. Hot soup, Gnauck's rocks with cheese spread, and hot coffee. Man, was lunch needed!

The afternoon was not nearly as scary, cold, or dreary as the morning. The fog had lifted, and the temperature increased. The wind and rain, however, remained. The afternoon was good only by comparison with the morning. We proceeded downstream, running all rapids we encountered. There was light conversation, and we were in good spirits. At 1515, we made camp. The sky lightened, and the sun came out in short five-minute bursts, only to be shut out as a series of nasty squall lines came through. We had dinner without the tarp, but no one ventured out fishing.

Thlewiaza-Seal Rivers: Challenge of the Ice

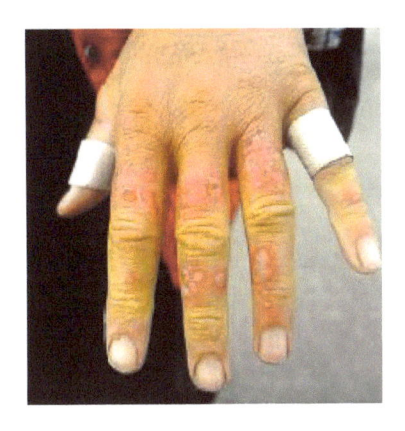

Gary's hands were in very bad shape from the blisters and cold. They were swollen and very sore.

We'd had two miserable days—yesterday on Shethanie Lake with the wind and today with fog, rain, and bone-chilling cold. Total distance covered today was thirty-one miles, mainly due to running all twelve rapids with no tip overs or portages. We were hoping for a break in the weather.

Chapter 20

A Continuation

Day 16: 4 July 1978

We were up at 0515 and on the water at 0735. The air temperature was 43°F; there was no fog, but the wind and rain had increased. The wind was still directly against us.

Gary became aware that, at some point yesterday, he'd hurt his left wrist and could not stroke at all; even a left draw was painful. Gary told Greg they should take obstacles on the right because he had minimum left movement capabilities.

Within the first fifteen minutes, when everyone was wet and felt miserable, we came upon the first whitewater of the day. The waves were four to six feet high with several rocks to avoid. Greg and Gary drew hard right to pass one rock, followed immediately by going right past the second. Left was the more prudent choice, but Gary didn't trust his wrist.

Our party stopped to check out a particularly rough-looking rapid. There was a sharp right turn, followed by very big waves. It looked like the best route was to take the center chute in the first part of the rapids and then move to the left to miss the really rough stuff downstream. The rapid was a classic and a good place for photographs, but the cold, rainy weather did not support this endeavor. We did not even attempt to retrieve our camera gear.

Brian and Carl went first; Greg and Gary followed, with Fred and Chuck at sweep. Each canoe was separated by about twenty yards. Gary looked ahead and could see Brian and Carl trying to pull out of the main channel. Greg and Gary were in the midst of big waves six to eight feet high. It was all Gary could do to hang in there and maintain balance. Gary yelled to Greg, "Left draw, hard!"

Gary looked ahead; there were a series of large standing waves at least eight to ten feet high, wild and furious. He was pulling on his left as hard as he could, totally forgetting about his wrist. The canoe wasn't responding! The river took command of the *Wakemaker II*. Gary saw a huge monster wave right ahead, and for the first time in his canoeing experience, he was immobilized by fear! This was not the "challenging" fear of earlier rapids, but a sick, give-in, we're-not-going-tomake- it fear. His is mind went blank momentarily while his body continued to paddle.

Three, possibly four-seconds passed, and the fate of the *Wakemaker II* was held in the balance. Then the mighty Seal River decided to let go, and Gary gained a measure of control. They slid off to the left of the monster wave. The fear was gone, and relief flooded his being.

Gary looked back; Fred and Chuck did not attempt a draw but took the big wave straight on. It looked like they were "goners" as the river had its way, but they hung in there and beat the waves fair and square. Some ride!

Sometime later, we came to the Great Island. The river split at this point into two channels, each going around the island some twenty miles long by eight miles wide. The main channel went to the right and consisted of many major rapids. Brian said there was one rapid that was very rough, so we needed to be careful. As we reached this section of the river, we encountered huge ice shelves along the banks of the river. These shelves were eight to ten feet high, forming solid ice cliffs. These cliffs made any sort of portage extremely difficult, if not impossible. We entered the first set of rapids with some trepidation, but they posed no problem. Further on, it got more difficult, and we pulled over to the side of the river and climbed up on the ice cliffs to get a better view. It was clear that we had to paddle upstream against the current for fifty yards and then ferry across the river to reach the only runnable chute. The whole operation looked formidable, yet we executed it like clockwork, and everyone got through without even a close call. Yet another ego builder!

We had another two-fire lunch without rain. Palls of steam rolled off our trousers and shirts. We all enjoyed the warmth provided by the fire. It was hard to put it out and go back to the cold, wet river. Lunch over, we hit the river with determination and renewed spirit. Then a fierce, twentyknot wind came up. It only lasted about forty-five minutes, but it was by far the hardest paddling of the entire trip. After Shethanie Lake, that was saying something. At the height of the blow, we saw a cow moose and her calf. They were on an island and headed for shore as we approach. The wind, rain, and fast current were almost too much for the calf, but the animal made it to shore safety.

We continued to encounter huge ice cliffs along the river at each rapid, forcing us to run the rapids blind. Fortunately, high water conditions allowed us to run all the rapids successfully. In low water, several of them might have been portages.

Brian cooked the "camp meal" which is a special meal prepared to celebrate the trip. Tonight, it was an incredible feast—three freeze-fried steaks per person, corn, rice, lasagna and meatballs, shrimp cocktail, dessert, and beverage. In spite of the cold and high energy output, we were absolutely stuffed. Brian's experience with ten years of wilderness camping really paid off when it came to food and cooking. Going too light can be a sad mistake, while taking too much food just adds to the burden; it's not easy to hit a happy medium.

Camp Meal. Three freeze dried steaks, wild rice, Lasagna & meat balls, shrimp cocktail, desert and beverage!

Chapter 21

Tundra

Day 17: 5 July 1978

At 0440, Brian and Gary watched a thunderstorm move over our campsite. Perhaps this was a good sign, an indication the weather was changing. The weather pattern was very turbulent and confused. It appeared that several different fronts were colliding over this part of Canada, and we were right in the middle. It rained for two hours, and then the weather began to break. We were on the water at 0700, in time to get wet; but shortly thereafter, the wind died down, and the rain stopped. The clouds were beginning to break up. As the morning progressed, the clouds continued to lift, and the sun came out in fits and starts. The wind picked up again, but nothing like we'd been experiencing. It was still cold, but no one was complaining.

The river continued to greet us with huge ten-to fifteen-foot ice shelves and an abundance of whitewater. We encountered one rapid that was nearly one mile long with large standing waves all the way. A rapid that was at least two miles long with big waves and rocks followed. The river was so big at this point we had no trouble running the rapids. There was always a chute or channel we could get through somewhere. Everyone had fun; there was enough challenge to keep us on our toes but no real danger.

Huge ice shelves along both shores

Huge ice shelves; Carl & Brian

Today we encountered our first seals. We were still a long way from

95

the ocean (over a hundred miles), and it was a little surprising to see them this far inland.

Navigation was quite different on this day; each stern man had his own map—the hand-drawn maps that Gary made at Treeline Lodge. These maps were no good for point-topoint navigation, but they did show the major bends in the river.

We made camp at 1500 on a large stretch of tundra, just up from a sandy beach on the river. Good river current, no portages, and only moderate wind, coupled with steady, hard paddling paid off.

Fred received a gold star. This afternoon, he delivered to Brian one can of beer and a recipe for making beer biscuits. He'd carried that can of beer all this way, through many temptations, particularly on some of those backbreaking portages. As this would likely be our last campsite with wood, we made a small baking fire and enjoyed beer biscuits. Indeed, they tasted like beer.

After taking a bath and washing some clothes, Gary, took a long walk into the tundra by himself—very strange, but fascinating; there were scattered clumps of forest remaining in isolated blocks maybe ten acres in size about four to ten miles apart. The forest stands were small, dwarfed, and ragged, the last remnants of the taiga. The area was full of potholes and small lakes, all at different elevations. Ponds only thirty feet apart had surface elevations of two to three feet difference. The area abounded with wildflowers and birds. It was a truly enjoyable hike. Gary walked approximately two miles and looked back toward camp. In the distance, Gary could see the two small, incredibly vulnerable tents and marveled at the fact that we'd made it this far. It seemed that, at any moment, the two blue specks would be swept away, and not even the call of the birds would mourn their passing.

The river trip was drawing to a close. Tomorrow, we expected to be at Hudson Bay, and that would end the river paddling. The trip had been super—save the bad weather during the previous five days. Yet, after one day of reasonably good paddling, the miseries of the earlier days began to fade from consciousness.

Chapter 22

Hudson Bay

Day 18: 6 July 1978

We were up at 0430. It was clear with a warm sun and no wind. Finally, after days of wet weather, we had a chance to dry out. Brian suggested we spread everything out and let it dry before tackling Hudson Bay. This plan was implemented and then quickly abandoned. By 0700, our party was on the water battling a strong wind and cold rain. Damn!

A beautiful morning on the tundra

It was again miserable. It was hard to paddle and hard to stay warm. The rain made what little navigation we had on the crude maps downright impossible, and so we just paddled on, not worrying about where we were. The countryside was completely tundra, and one bend in the river looked just like the next. Nothing on the map looked anything like what we were paddling through. We estimated our speed at six plus miles per hour and used time as a measure of distance.

Lunch was on a point of land covered by dense willow. In addition to collecting wood for the noon fire, we loaded up the canoes with extra wood for the trek down the bay. Brian brought his Phoebes stove to use for cooking, but it was not adequate to warm all of us. We needed a wood fire to help us dry out. If this weather continued, we'd need the wood; that was for sure.

After lunch, the river changed drastically. It broke up into a delta. There were dozens of "main" channels going off in different directions. We tried to follow what appeared to be the biggest channel, but that was not always clear. Each channel became its own "river." The "rivers" merged, split, merged, and split again and again. As we approached the bay, we negotiated several miles of intermittent rock-dodging rapids, alternating with fast current and standing waves. Finally, after quite a long time, we caught our first glimpse of Hudson Bay.

Living in the San Francisco Bay Area, Gary had come to know and love the ocean. The sight of this huge, endless body of water was indeed welcomed. As we neared Hudson Bay, we tried to gauge how far we should go. We did not want to go past the last suitable campsite, for that might mean sleeping the night in the canoe on a mud flat. Fred and Gary became concerned we were reaching the point of "no return" and opted to haul out. We found a small bay to wait while Brian and Gary scouted ahead from a high point of land.

Brian and Gary walked about three-quarters of a mile to the end of a rocky point. It was clear we still had about a mile and half of river left. The mighty Seal completed its journey with a series of large rapids, and then it was absorbed by the even mightier Hudson Bay. Brian felt very strongly we should camp below the big rapids, where we could monitor the tides and would have only a very small stretch of river in the morning.

They looked over the rapids from where we stood, about a quarter of a mile away. The rapids appeared to be big but nothing the Thlewiaza, Booth, or Seal Rivers had shown us. They had not been sufficient to stop this crew, and it wasn't likely the last rapids would either.

All agreed with the suggestion to move downriver. We realized it was a good tactic so loaded up the canoes and shoved off. Our canoes were loaded down with a lot of extra wood, and they were sluggish.

These rapids were, by far, the biggest any of us had ever gone through. Both Fred and Gary told of their experience of running these rapids. Gary's description is first:

> The rapids started much the same as the previous ones on the Seal, but it quickly became very rough and unmanageable. I looked ahead and saw Brian and Carl really having trouble. Right then, Greg and I hit some very large standing waves head-on. They were a good eight to ten feet high, and there were five or six of them. Had it not been for the decking, we would have swamped as the water broke over the canoe. We barely had control of the canoe, and the river was tossing us around pretty much at will. The Seal was not about to let us off easily. We straightened the canoe out, and I began to get a sense of the river when I heard Greg yell, "*Oh, my God!*"
>
> Immediately ahead was the largest set of waves I had run on any river. We were being sucked into a monstrous V-shaped wave. The wave

on the right was a ten-to-twelve-foot green giant, dwarfed only by the left wave. The wave on the left was fifteen feet from base to crest. We are going to hit the "V" at the apex, I thought. No, the left wave was much stronger; we were hitting it three-quarters on the port side

There was no doubt in my mind or in Greg's; we had bought the farm! Strangely, though concerned, I did not experience the morbid fear of several days earlier in waves considerably smaller.

The wave broke over the *Wakemaker II* and flipped the canoe over like a toy. It was green all over and cold, sending a shock through my entire system. I was underwater for several seconds and then popped to the surface and experienced a secondary scare. I could not find the stern rope, and my left hand was only lightly resting on the bottom of the canoe. The current was pulling the canoe away from me, and there was nothing I could hang onto. I did not want to lose the canoe at all cost.

The first rule of canoeing in a tip over is to stay with the canoe. The second rule is to hang onto your paddle. The canoe floated out of reach just as I came up from underneath. In a desperate attempt to get back to the canoe I let go of my paddle and reached for Greg's hand. He was able to pull me back and I got a good grip on the canoe. Just then, Fred and Chuck arrived. They were behind us going down the rapids and saw us go over. I yelled to them to snag my paddle, that we are all right and would meet up below.

The immediate area was filled with rocks, waves, and strong current; it was too difficult to execute any sort of rescue. We rode the rapids out until we reached several large, flat rocks above water level and stopped. Brian and Carl hopped over the rocks and helped us right the canoe. I made an equipment check and found that nothing was lost except the bailing bucket, my map, and some wood, which Chuck and Fred were retrieving. The rear decking flap was torn off, apparently when we tipped over. Other than that, everything was intact.

We were some distance from where Brian wanted to camp but thought it best to paddle on. This entailed navigating a few small rock-dodging rapids.

Fred described how he and Chuck survived the rapids:

Chuck and I agreed that it would be better to run the rapids before making camp. My impression was that the rapids were not extremely big. As a result, neither Chuck nor I paid much attention to fastening the decking down, but as we came out of the bay where we were waiting, I could see that the rapids were big. I yelled to Chuck to make sure his decking was secure because it looked really bad downriver. We passed through some big, about eight feet high, standing waves, and then the river just dropped about 20 feet out of sight—not over a water falls, but down about a 45-degree slope. On the other side of the drop was a huge standing wave that formed a "V" in the middle. The wave was bigger than any I had ever seen.

I could see the stern of Brian's canoe just as it disappeared from sight as it went over the top of the standing wave. It appeared that they were going to make it. Gary, on the other hand, was about 15 feet to the left, and I watched as the top of the standing wave hit his canoe from a quartering angle, which rolled Gary's canoe. I knew that Gary and Greg had no chance and were over.

About this time, Chuck turned around and yelled, "How are we going to run this?"

I yelled back, "Straight down the middle, go for the center of the "V."

Chuck did a magnificent job of hitting the center of the "V" but was about a foot left of center. Chuck was struck full on from his head to his waist by the wave as we knifed through the "V." Since we slightly missed the center of the "V," the canoe rolled, and Chuck had all he could do to prevent the canoe from rolling completely over.

I was oblivious to this because I had problems of my own. Because we were slightly left of the "V" center, the left side of the standing wave broke over the canoe behind Chuck, followed immediately by the right side of the standing wave. As a result, a seven-foot-long by about two-foot-high wall of water cane across the top of the canoe and hit me with a crushing blow. The water knocked me flat on the stern of the canoe and tried to wrench the paddle out of my hand, but I was able to hold on. I was able to keep from being washed out of the canoe only because my foot came up on the bow side of the thwart when the water hit me.

Once I could regain paddling position, I could see that Chuck had everything under control and that the canoe was steady as a rock. Chuck was leaning forward in the bow ready to do battle with the standing waves below. Chuck had been able to keep the canoe from rolling over and it was time for me to help him.

When I saw that our canoe was safe, I turned my attention to the others. I could see that Brian and Carl had landed on a large flat rock and were ready to throw Gary and Greg a rope. Gary and Greg were safely holding on their canoe and the current was pushing them toward the rock where Brian and Carl were standing. Since it was apparent that the rest were safe, Chuck and I went around picking up the map, paddles, some wood and other objects that fell out of Gary's canoe. This was difficult because the current was fast and there were many rocks to maneuver around, but we had no mishap and soon joined the others on the rock.

Greg and Gary were cold; it had been about twenty minutes from the time they'd tipped over until we were ready to shove off. Both of them were severely chilled, but paddling hard warmed them some. We made it to a campsite near Hudson Bay without further mishap. A hot fire plus a change of clothes (the waterproof dry bags held up well) helped enormously. The river temperature was 57°F; had a similar tip over occurred earlier in the trip, it would have been a lot more serious.

Campfire conversations alternated between reliving the great tip over to planning for the next day. Gary did not feel at all bad about not being able to take the huge V-shaped wave. Brian and Fred felt lucky to have made it. What Gary was mad about was not having scouted the rapids in detail before making the run. Even a cursory evaluation would have identified the monster wave. We could have run the rapids father to the right side in "calm" (only eight-foot) waves and, in all likelihood, made it OK. That would have given the party a perfect record. Instead, overconfidence, fueled by the ego-building runs of the past three weeks, had ruled. Gary really had not believed the Seal River could throw us a rapid we couldn't handle—dumb, dumb, dumb!

So much for the great tip over. Now how about Hudson Bay? The plan was to watch the tide and leave on the next incoming tide. Then, depending on what we found, we would either try to go out beyond the low tide mark (about six miles) and stay on the bay until the next high tide (twelve hours) or play it close to shore and camp as soon as the tide began to recede. The latter plan didn't sound practical, as it would give us a two to three-hour shot paddling at high tide. At this point, we did not know what to expect. As a result of running the last rapids, we'd gained a new respect for the water and were not about to take unnecessary chances.

Chapter 23

The Ordeal

Day 19 and 20: 7-8 July 1978

We were all up early in anticipation of the Hudson Bay. The weather was not good—39°F with a fifteen- to eighteen-knot wind from the West. The water temperature was 50°F in the river and probably a lot colder in the Bay proper. Brian was antsy; he wanted to move out at 0700; Fred wanted to wait until 0900. Finally, at 0830, we decided to move. It was very exciting. We still had about half a mile of rock-dodging rapids to run until we got to the open water. We navigated the rapids in normal style (not the great tip over style) and made a sharp right turn, paddling due south once we left the last of the river current. As we proceeded, we become aware of the strength of the wind. In the shallow (four- to ten-feet-deep) mud flats, the fifteen-knot wind produced very treacherous, choppy waves. Gary had experienced similar waves a number of times when paddling in San Francisco Bay. His remedy there was to turn around and go home.

Brian and Carl were paddling about half a mile out from shore, Greg and Gary about 250 yards out. Greg was totally unfamiliar with ocean waves and how to work them. These waves were not over four feet high, but they were quite different from the standing waves encountered in rapids. A standing wave is just that; it stays in one place, and the canoe moves through it or over it. In the ocean, the waves move along, against, with, or broadside to the canoe. The balance and stroking were quite different. Greg wanted no part of these Hudson Bay waves. Fred and Chuck did not cotton one iota to the idea of riding them for twelve hours. Gary didn't feel uncomfortable with the waves themselves, but he didn't like the wind. If we got too far out, say four or five miles, and had to come in to camp, we would be working directly against the wind and waves. If the wind increased, we would not be able to paddle against it. Paddling broadside was hard enough. Fred was concerned Brian and Carl were already too far out. If the wind increased much more, vigorous paddling would only maintain their position; eventually, they would tire, and the wind would wash them farther out to sea. If this sounds dramatic and unreal, it is suggested the reader try paddling into a fifteen-knot wind with a loaded canoe. It isn't easy.

All three canoes proceeded south in about the same positions. Suddenly, Greg gasped, "Look at that!"

Two huge, white Beluga whales surfaced twenty feet away and then dove and surfaced again a few feet on the other side of the canoes. About a hundred yards out, they turned around and repeated the maneuver and then repeated it one more time. It would have been frightening had we not known what they were. Even so, it was nerve-racking to think that even a slight miscalculation on their part would dump us into the icy water. Gary wanted to take a photograph, but to wait out just the right second when they surfaced simply couldn't be done. The strong wind demanded constant attention to the balance and orientation of the canoe. Even a few seconds of not paddling could cause problems.

It wasn't long before we realized the tide was going out! Since we were closer to shore, we realized the change sooner than Brian. We tried to signal Brian, but he didn't want to come in. We were in a small bay where rocks and debris were becoming visible directly ahead and strung out to the left closer to where Brian and Carl were paddling. Finally, they realized what was happening and came in.

Waiting for the tide to come in

At 1100, we pitched the tents, started a small fire, and discussed our options. They were few. The weather had clouded up, the wind had increased, and it was beginning to rain again. Everyone went back into the tents. There was a major disagreement as to how far we had come. Gary's hand-drawn maps were very crude, but Gary was sure we had only made about six miles from the mouth of the Seal. Brian and Fred believed we were twice that distance. That meant we'd averaged seven miles an hour! Gary could accept this figure going with the wind but not broadside to it.

The plan was to wait out the wind, the rain, and the tide and proceed again at 2100. This would give us just two hours of paddling before darkness set in and the tide went out again. If the weather held, we would have to limit our paddling to a two- to three-hour block right at high tide; no one wanted to tackle Hudson Bay for twelve hours in this wind. We were all glad we had three full days to get to Churchill.

Inside the tent was warm and cozy; outside it was bitter cold and wet. The wind continued to get stronger, and in mid-afternoon Brian took a reading—twenty-five to twenty-seven knots due west. There were several times throughout the afternoon when it really looked like the tents were going to blow away. This was perhaps the most frightening thought of the trip. We did not want to think about the consequences.

Hilton Inn on Hudson Bay

Dinner was cooked inside the six-man tent on Brian's Phoebus stove. We also made up an emergency food pack for each person. We place several "Gnauck rocks," a can of sardines, beef jerky, and an energy bar inside

Diner on Hudson Bay

large waterproof plastic containers. These food packs were to be opened only if it became necessary to eat on the run out in Hudson Bay.

Breaking camp had to be timed just right. If we broke early, we would be standing around in the rain waiting for the tide to come in. If we waited too long, we would lose precious paddling time. We hit the water at 2115 and began poking our way out to sea. The wind had quieted to around fifteen knots, but the rain and cold continued. The air temperature was 41°F and the water temperature was 38° F; the situation was not to be taken lightly.

All three canoes pushed father out this time, maybe a mile from shore. We occasionally ran into very shallow areas full of rocks and boulders. These shallows made canoeing almost impossible. We found it much harder to navigate a boulder field in the wind-swept choppy water of Hudson Bay than in boulder-strewn rapids. No one wanted to tip over! So, we moved father out into deeper water. Although the waves were bigger, it was much safer and easier to paddle. Along about 2300 we began to look for a place to camp. We angled in toward shore. As we moved closer to shore, we again encountered extensive boulder fields that slowed progress, but it was getting dark. We were headed toward what looked like high ground about a quarter mile away.

At 2330 Fred exclaimed, "The tide is going out. We better find a place soon or live in the canoe for the night."

Everyone was very cold, wet, tired, and hungry. We'd had enough paddling for one day, and all we could think about was getting a fire going (if there was enough wood), getting something to eat, and hitting the sack.

As we approach the rock-strewn shore in the dim twilight, Gary thought he saw something over his right shoulder near shore. Gary looked again and could not see anything, so we continued. The water was about eighteen inches deep, and we were still 150 yards from shore. If we didn't want a long, hard portage to shore, we had better hurry.

Again, Gary caught a faint glimpse of movement off to his right. Gary looked again but still made nothing out of the dark gray landscape. At seventy-five yards, we were in eight inches of water. It looked like we were going to have to make some type of portage. Then Gary looked a third time and saw something move from right to left, directly in front of us. It was a huge, whitish blob.

Gary desperately strained to get a better look in the rapidly fading light. The animal was momentarily silhouetted against the last remnants of light in the western sky. Gary saw the unmistakable outline and gait of a bear. It was a polar bear! An exchange of comments then followed:

"Look there," Gary yelled. "There—it's a polar bear!" It was hard to express the shock, fear, and downright dismay Gary felt at this moment.

"What?"

"Huh, where? I don't see anything."

"Are you kidding?"

"Right there," Gary yelled, pointing his paddle, "right on shore. No, he's going inland now. No wait; now he's coming back. He's pacing back and forth. Right there. See him?"

"I still don't see him," said Greg.

"Nor I," said Fred.

Carl spoke. "I see something moving, but I can't tell what it is."

"I can. It's a bear; I know it," Gary countered. "But I can't see him now; it's getting too dark. He's been following us the last hundred yards." Gary saw him before, but now he was no longer sure.

"What do we do now?" someone asked.

That was a very good question, and it occupied our attention for the next few minutes. A decision had to be made now! The tide was rapidly going out. There were three options:(1) tackle the bear head-on and scare him off, (2) tackle the bay at night in a storm, or (3) make no decision, let the tide go out, wait for the bear to walk out to us, and let him decide. There were no good or pleasant choices. It was clearly a matter of picking the least of three evils.

The last option was really not acceptable to any of us, so we quickly decided; it would be the bay. Knowledge was the deciding factor. As risky and dangerous as the bay would be in this weather, we knew we had a chance—slim, maybe, but it was there. If no one lost his cool and if the wind did not get worse or a sneaker wave did not tip the canoes, we could do it.

The bear, on the other hand, represented a complete unknown. A black bear can be frightened off; a grizzly would probably have ignored us unless he felt threatened. A polar bear was another matter; they had been known to stalk men who were hunting them. Further, we knew before embarking on the trip that there was a very high concentration of polar bears in the vicinity of Churchill. The polar bears had become a nuisance. They had learned that man means garbage, which means food, and frequently entered Churchill in the winter (they don't hibernate). There were numerous stories of bears raiding campsites in search of food. If this bear was bent on getting our grub, there was no way we could stop him. At the very least, he would tear up the gear and eat the food (very bad), perhaps put a hole in one of the canoes (worse), and even take to tasting people (really terrible). On the other hand, there were a number of stories about polar bears walking into camps and walking out without even nosing around.

Perhaps we could yell, scream, bang the canoes, and wave the paddles and scare the bear out of our campsite. Even a polar bear would think twice about taking on six screaming maniacs. But what if he didn't? What if he came back in the middle of the night when we were sleeping? What if he had a bad tooth and didn't give a damn? Did we make the right decision?

Decision made, it was time to execute the plan and quickly head out. If we did not make it past the low tide line, there would be nothing to keep the bear from walking out to where we were and doing his thing.

With the wind at our back and paddling furiously, we headed due east and reached deep water in fifteen minutes. The swells in the bay were big! The waves were six to seven feet high with an occasional white cap. Gary was concerned more than ever about the wind. It was taking us straight east out into Hudson Bay. Churchill was to the southeast of our location. Once committed to the bay, it was only logical to set a course for Churchill. We could not see any sense fighting the wind and rain for nothing.

After a few minutes of paddling east with the wind at our backs (we were really flying), we changed course and paddled due south, paralleling the shore—the theory being, if we paddled south and the wind pushed us east, the resulting vector would be southeast. Gary was the only one with a workable oil-damped compass and so led. (Brian had an air-damped compass that would not stabilize because of the low gravitational signal this far north.) The waves were at the limit of what experienced paddlers in a decked canoe could handle. There was no margin for error. We had to watch closely for sneaker waves, turn the canoe into the wave, ride them out, and turn again toward the south. To take these big waves broadside was to invite disaster. Gary became very concerned the wind was blowing us ten feet due east for each three feet we paddled south. This was a frightening thought, for if true, we could miss Churchill completely. The next point of civilization after Churchill was over four hundred miles away.

We wanted to stay close together in case of a tip over and to be able to communicate. Twenty yards was optimum. Any closer reduced our maneuvering room and made everyone nervous. Farther away made it hard to hear each other.

The hours passed and we were all very cold and very tired; still, we kept paddling. There was no choice. We saw many whales and quite a few flocks of ducks and geese. It would have been fascinating if the whole thing wasn't so serious and we weren't so tired. The minutes and miles passed, and all the while, we were concerned about the wind pushing us too far east.

At 0200, Greg exclaimed, "Hey, we're in shallow water!"

We checked. And sure enough, it was only three feet deep! That simply could not be. If Gary's navigation was even generally correct, there was no way we could be anywhere near shore, and yet we were clearly in shallow water. At this point, the wind died down and was in the process of changing directions. The water was becoming a confusion of waves going every which way. Gary had lost track of his internal north reference.

Gary didn't know where we were or which way to go. Having lost his west wind reference, it was necessary to check the heading of the canoe every few strokes. It was dark and Gary had to hold his compass very close to his face to get a reading. In the interim the canoe kept changing course and floated around aimlessly. It was hard to get on track again. Gary had lost faith in the compass! It always seemed to be pointing south. If it was wrong, we were totally lost and in deep trouble.

The other two canoes were separated from Greg and Gary by about fifty yards. They were trying to follow Gary and had no idea what Gary was doing. As they paddled hard to catch up, Gary told Greg he wanted to check the compass heading. They turned their canoe 180° around and paddled due north. Gary checked to see what the compass read. At this point, the other two canoes arrived. The *Harricana VI* and HMS *Victory* were going south, and the *Wakemaker II* slid between them, going north. The other four men were totally beside themselves with frustration and dismay as they watched the *Wakemaker II* head for Eskimo Point.

Someone yelled, "What way are we going?"

Gary yelled back, "South, but I'm going north."

"He's flipped his wig, gone crazy," said Carl. Suddenly the irony of it hit Carl, and he broke into peals of laughter.

We all saw the comic element in the situation and joined in. Carl, in particular, thought it was the damnedest thing he had ever experienced and could tell this part of the story better than anyone else.

We pulled the three canoes together and again discussed our plight. It was clear we couldn't go further south for the water had become too shallow. We changed course and headed due east, checking the water depth as we went. The humor faded, and a cold, quiet despair fell over the party. There were few words spoken and only to check on direction or to confirm everyone was OK.

Things looked very bleak, and we all knew the seriousness of the situation. No one said anything, but we knew that, if there was a tip over, the chances of the other two canoes affecting a rescue were very, very poor. Even if we could get to the other persons, haul them into the canoes without causing another tip over (and that was a big if), there was no way we could get them into dry clothes and near a fire. Hypothermia would set in shortly. In fact, we were beginning to worry about hypothermia as it was. Everyone was very cold, as we had been up since early the previous morning. Fortunately, at this point, everyone seemed to be all right. Gary was particularly impressed with Chuck. At seventeen, he was taking on physical and emotional stress that would be difficult for many men to handle.

Just as we were about to lose all hope, Greg yelled, "Look, there are lights!"

My God, he was right. Ahead, not more than a forty-five-minute paddle, were lights. Brian and Fred reasoned they must be lights of the big grain elevators in Churchill. (They had both been to Churchill before.) Eureka, we had found it! There had never been a happier bunch of fellows on the seven seas than the six of us at this moment. Shouts of joy broke forth and filled the air. A hot bath in Churchill was something to look forward to. We forgot all about our cold and fatigue and really set to at a vigorous pace—due east toward the lights. We were soon out in deep water with very big swells running to eight feet. With the wind almost directly on our backs, we were making good time.

We followed the lights for forty minutes with high spirits and joy in our hearts. Strangely, the lights seemed no closer than when we'd started; that was puzzling and disappointing. We figured we were doing at least seven miles an hour, and we should have reached them by now. Then as we looked, the lights faded, grew dim, flickered, and went out! Stunned silence came over the crew.

We continued east for another twenty minutes without saying a word. Everyone was scared. Gary experienced a kind of fear never experienced before. We were lost, cold, and tired and on the verge of losing control. Gary again became concerned about going too far east. Gary even doubted that the lights we had been following were real. They may have been an illusion or possibly a passing ship. We knew toward the south was land, and Gary suggested we go for it. Fred and Greg felt we should continue east, but neither felt strongly enough to press the point or take the compass and lead the way. At this point, Gary would gladly follow someone who said, "Give me the compass, Gary. I know how to get us out of this mess."

We turned south and paddled until 0530 when we came to a small, exposed rocky shoal. Fred paddled over to Brian and said, "Brian, there's an island over there. Let's stop and stretch our legs."

Brian said, "I don't see an island. I think you're hallucinating."

Fred replied, "Brian, there's an island over there, and I'm going to stretch my legs."

Fortunately, the others followed. The island was perhaps three acres in size and just a mass of rocks and boulders, but it was land, and it felt good to walk about.

Brian and Gary tried to light the Phoebus stove, but Gary's fingers were so numb that he could not flip the Bic lighter. Brian tried to light farmer (strike-anywhere) matches to no avail. Fred was approaching hypothermia, having lost all feeling in his feet; he was so cold he could not get his backpack opened to retrieve some thermal underwear. Carl approached Fred and asked if he could have his tent for a shelter. Fred told him he could have it if he could get his pack open. Chuck and Greg went to help Carl set the tent up. Gary still felt OK, although wet and cold, but his hands were totally numb. It was clear; if this ordeal went on much longer, we were going to be past the limit.

Brian took the stove into the tent and was able to light it and run it full blast in the tent. We broke out the emergency food kits. Thank God and Brian for thinking ahead. This bit of food plus the stove was enough to get everyone back to life again.

Just as we were about to get warm and think more clearly, Chuck looked out the door and yelled, "Hey, the tide's coming in. One of the canoes is free!"

There was a mad scramble to get organized, so we could get underway. Gary dashed out and grabbed the canoe in about eight inches of water. A few more minutes, and it would have been gone.

We'd taken the tent down, stowed the gear, and were about to get underway when someone looked up and saw a tall structure on the horizon. It was getting light now, and there was no mistaking this for an illusion; the structure looked like the Churchill grain elevators. Everyone looked and verified they could see it. Yes, it was real. Or at least it looked real; it must be Churchill. It was only forty to forty-five minutes away (interestingly that's how far away the structure had been three hours ago).

Brian had Gary took a bearing lest they disappear like the lights did last night. Gary did— almost due east, maybe 85°.

We piled into the canoes and started out with renewed hope. The rain had stopped, but the wind had picked up and was blowing from the northwest. To maintain a true easterly bearing, we had to paddle northeast. The waves hit us broadside three-quarters to the stern, a difficult angle to maintain and one that was hard to balance properly. We paddled for two hours and were no closer to the structures than before; it was very frustrating, and no one could really understand it. It always looked just a little way away.

Now a cloud settled down over the water; the fine, misty rain started again; and the structure disappeared. Undoubtedly, this was what had happened the night before. We waited patiently for the cloud to rise and the structure to appear again so we could see our destination.

After an hour, the cloud passed; the structure was gone, simply vanished! We could make out a shoreline on the horizon but no man-made structure. It was very frustrating and very disconcerting. Our goal was so real and vivid one minute, and it was completely gone the next.

A new problem haunted the crew; the shoreline consisted of sheer rock cliffs—50 to 150 feet high. Huge breakers crashed on the rocks. Any canoe would be smashed to pieces in a few seconds if it got caught in the surf, and all in the canoe would be killed. We paddled along the shore toward the southeast, staying well away from shore. Finally, after about three hours of paddling, we saw a small break in the rocky shore, a small bay, and a beach suitable to land on.

Upon beaching the canoes, we saw some type of emergency shelter. It was fully stocked with food inside and litter strewn about outside. We had tents and plenty of food, so there was no need to break in. If we became marooned here, at least we could last a long time.

Camp was way up the hillside in the worst place of the whole trip. It was the best campsite we could find, and no one complained in the least. Brian, Greg, and Gary climbed to the top of a large hill to look around (Fred, Chuck, and Carl could think of nothing but sleep). Dense fog covered the area, and nothing could be seen, so they returned to camp. Everyone was operating on terrible nervous energy, but it was time to get some rest. Our tent was pitched on a jumble of rocks, but it was OK. In a few minutes Gary was nearly asleep when he heard the sound of a jet airplane and thought we had to be near Churchill.

Two hours later, Brian woke us up. "Time to get up; we have a ride into Churchill." he said.

It turned out Brian hadn't slept much. After an hour, he' woken up and again climbed the hill to see if he could get a bearing on exactly where we were and the most expeditious way to get to Churchill. The hill provided a vantage point. Below was the Churchill River, and beyond it, the city of Churchill. It was still about ten miles away via Hudson Bay, nearly a full day paddle. On the way back to camp, Brian checked on the canoes and found several young fishermen nearby. One volunteered to pull us into Churchill later in the afternoon after he'd checked on his nets. We had two hours to eat our last camp meal and get ready for the tow. We had a double portion of everything, including dessert. The food plus the nap revived everyone.

Two hours later, the young fishermen, Arnold Brauner and a native Indian friend arrived. They had a large boat with a 25-horsepower Johnson motor. Our three bowmen rode in the boat and drank beer and whiskey, while the three stern men stayed with the canoes to keep them in line. Gary's rope was attached to a point on the boat, Fred's bow rope was hooked to Gary's stern, and Brian brought up the rear. The ride back was fun and took about an hour, even with an outboard at full power. Chuck, at seventeen, was having fun drinking Arnold's beer and offering the bottle to his dad, knowing full well that Fred could not reach the beer. Arnold's Indian friend would grab a wiggling fish out of the bait box and drop it into his mouth for a snack once in a while. He would offer one to Chuck, but he declined, favoring his beer.

Free ride to Churchill

Arnold was a really nice guy and helped us stow the gear and gave us a ride into town. He would not accept any money but suggested we could meet him at the bar later in the evening.

After checking into the hotel, all of us took hot, hot baths and just sort of soaked for a while. Everyone was thankful we'd made it without any serious mishap. After cleaning up and changing clothes, we had a second huge dinner at the local restaurant.

Later we meet Arnold, his wife, his Indian friend, and his buddies in the local bar. They were very friendly, but we were in for a culture shock. The environment was rough, and the people who lived here were rough, too. They had developed their own speech pattern, and although they spoke a form of English, it took some getting used to. The most common letter in their alphabet was "u". That was because the most common word was a four-letter one beginning with "f." A typical greeting might go something like this, 'Hi, you G— d— mo—f—r, I'll buy you son of a b— a f— ing drink.' Both men and women were easy with the foul language, yet they meant no harm. The words were not always used in the foul sense but as handy, unconscious modifiers to nouns and verbs.

The evening fun, financed by our party, was well worth the price. Everyone had a good time. At one point, Arnolds' wife was having an altercation with another woman, and believe it or not, they went out back to settle their differences. This did not faze Arnold one bit. He said, "My wife can take care of herself," and continued having fun.

We turned in at midnight and felt very thankful that we were all safe and sound. It was hard to believe, a few hours before, the fate of our small party hung in the balance, between a glorious, victorious finish and a dreadful, terrible tragedy.

Chapter 24

Return and Reflection

Day 21: 9 July 1978

There was no urgency or need to arise early, as we had nothing planned until 1000 in the morning, yet Gary was up and out of bed (notice, Gary said bed) at 0630. He took a stroll to look over the environs of Churchill. A small, remote wilderness town, it was hard to see how its 1,700 inhabitants made a living and, even more, why they chose to stay. Surely, material wealth was not the attraction; nor was it the beauty of the surrounding countryside, as it was flat and uninteresting. The town itself possessed neither the charm nor setting seen at Lynn Lake, yet Churchill was the major supply depot for dozens of small settlements that dotted the North Country. Grain grown in central Canada was brought to Churchill, stored in huge containers, and then shipped to other parts of the world when the Hudson Bay was free of ice. In its way, Churchill represented an important link to the modern world.

Breakfast, at the local restaurant, occurred in two shifts —the early risers and the late risers. It included, for almost everyone, several large glasses of fresh milk, a luxury we did not have on the water.

Churchill

We planned, through the graciousness of Arnold Brauner who was to act as our guide, a trip to the Fort Prince of Wales National Monument. It is a huge structure located across the Churchill River on a large peninsula. The fort, built during the heydays of the Hudson Bay Company and its rivals, represented a vast and fascinating history.

An interesting event occurred during our trip to the fort, for, at least in part, it supported our decision to canoe Hudson Bay and not have the face-off against the bear. The previous night, we'd recounted our adventure with the polar bear to Arnold. He boldly claimed we could easily have scared the bear by beating two pans together. Hearing this, Gary began to doubt the wisdom of our decision.

Well, it seemed that people were not the only creatures who visit the fort. Polar bears were very common. Any official tour must have the protection offered by a guard carrying a 12- gauge shotgun. Private parties were advised to take a weapon. The clincher came when we all met at the marina and piled into Arnold's boat for a ride over the Churchill River to the Fort. Who arrived with a high-powered rifle in hand? Yes, indeed, it was none other than Arnold Brauner himself. Fred asked him why he didn't have a couple of pans rather than a high-powered rifle. Arnold did not reply, at least not out loud.

Fred held the rifle while Arnold maned the motor.

Our flight back to Lynn Lake arrived in the afternoon. We were packed and ready to go. Parson Air had chosen a single-engine Otter for the return flight, and there was ample room for all. As we passed over Button Bay shortly after takeoff, it was warm and sunny. The bay was at low tide, exposing the vast tidal flats. As We looked at the bay, it was hard to comprehend the fear and helplessness we felt some fourteen hours earlier. The bay was now calm, benign, and very quiet.

Button Bay of Hudson Bay at low tide. A stormy night was spent here.

The flight was two and a half hours long, and we were at an altitude of only four thousand feet. In all that time, we never saw a trail, road, or a single sign of man. This was literally impossible anywhere in the United States other than Alaska, which represents the western extremity of the same wilderness.

The Thlewiaza-Seal River canoe trip was truly a canoe adventure. Gary captured the essence of the adventure in the final section of the log he wrote shortly after completing the trip. In honor of Gary, this book is ended with his reflections:

Thlewiaza-Seal Rivers: Challenge of the Ice

    I think about our entire trip beginning with the early news of the ice, our first rapids, the long portages around Kashmere Falls, the ice on Kashmere Lake, the grizzly, the many rapids, my big fish, and the reunion with Dad at Nueltin Lake. I remembered too, our trek south via the Booth River to the big lakes, the big rapids of the North Seal and then the change of weather, the days of cold, wet hard paddling, the final send-off the Seal River gave us as we entered Hudson Bay and finally the ordeal on Hudson Bay. It has been intense and very fulfilling. I realize how fortunate I am to have experienced this firsthand. I vow, God willing, that I will return to the North Country to savor once again the cold, clear water, green forest, and blue sky.

Epilogue

Closing Comments by the Author, Fred E. Nelson

November 2020

Brian Gnauck holds the trip record for our group by completing at least fifty wilderness canoe trips in Canada between his first wilderness trip on the Harricana River in 1970 and 2019 when he died. His bowman, Carl Schmieder, completed fifteen wilderness canoe trips, starting with the Harricana River in 1970. Most of these trips were with Brian, but a few were with me. I hold second place with nineteen wilderness canoe trips in Canada, starting with my first trip on the Missinaibi River in 1969. I still take one or two local canoe trips a year, but at eighty-seven, for me, the Canadian wilderness trips are too much now. My bowman and son, Chuck took five wilderness canoe trips with his dad. He canoes frequently but does not like to take wilderness trips without his dad. Gary participated in at least nine wilderness canoe trips before he died in 2019. We lost contact with Greg Dufeck, Gary's bowman on the Thlewiaza-Seal River trip.

The Thlewiaza-Seal Rivers canoe trip took place from mid-June to mid-July 1978. Gary volunteered to write the log of the trip with inputs from the other canoeists. The technology available at the time was very old. Those were the days when the film with the photos taken on the trip was sent to a company for developing and producing prints. Gary had a word processor to help with creating and formatting the text, but the photos had to be glued in place by hand. Although Gary only charged each canoeist for his out-of-pocket costs, the album still cost several hundred dollars. No one complained about the cost because the album provided the catalyst for reliving an adventure that all of us enjoyed.

I received a call from Gary in 2004 to ask if I still had the slides taken on the canoe trip. Gary explained that he was going to redo the log using the advanced technology available at the time. He called again several months later to say that the album was finished and was checking to see if I wanted the revised edition because the price was still going to be several hundred dollars. The album was breathtaking. It was the same size as the original, twelve by sixteen inches, but Gary enlarged some of the impressive photos to the full twelve by sixteen inches. The result was truly a work of art.

My wife, Mary Jean, never had an interest in reading the logs of the wilderness canoe trips in Canada. But she was not feeling well in January 2019 and was looking for something exciting to read, so I gave her Gary's revised log to read. I was pleased to see that she started to read the log in the afternoon but was surprised to have her return it the next evening, so I asked if she had read all of it. She said that she could not put it down until the end. This comment convinced me that the log should be published as a book so other people could enjoy reading about our adventure in the comfort of their homes.

I tried calling and e-mailing Gary to discuss publishing the log as a book without success. I could not contact his brother, Brian, because he'd died in 2019. However, I was able to contact Brian's wife, who told me that Gary had also died in 2019 and gave me the phone number of Gary's daughter. Gary's daughter was delighted that I wanted to publish the log as a book.

Our party was very fortunate that this trip had a good ending. Had any number of events unfolded slightly differently, the ending would likely have been very tragic. It is not an exaggeration to say that obituaries for all six people may well have been written. Call it what you will, a guardian angel, fate, or just dumb luck—we survived.

To those readers new to wild river canoeing, recognize the Thlewiaza-Seal Rivers expedition reflects the extremes of this sport. Most wilderness canoe trips, while arduous and physically demanding, do not represent a material threat to life, limb, or property. So many little things had to work out just right for us, or you would not be reading this book. Since "all is well that ends well," you are able to read about the most exciting and cherished experiences of our lives. One does not know beforehand which trip will be something outside the norm. If you choose to participate, be prepared! Read, learn, and enjoy.

You might be curious about Gary's rash. As noted in the book, Gary developed a very severe rash during the Thlewiaza-Seal Rivers trip. He saw a doctor as soon as he returned home, but the doctor could not do anything because the rash had completely disappeared between the time the canoe trip ended and when he saw a doctor. The canoeists on the next trip discussed this rash at great length to determine possible causes. The use of DEET was put on the top of the list of possible causes. We set about verifying this hypothesis by asking anyone using DEET on their skin who started to get a rash to stop using DEET. This procedure was used on several trips, and each time, the rash cleared up in a couple of days after the person stopped applying DEET on skin.

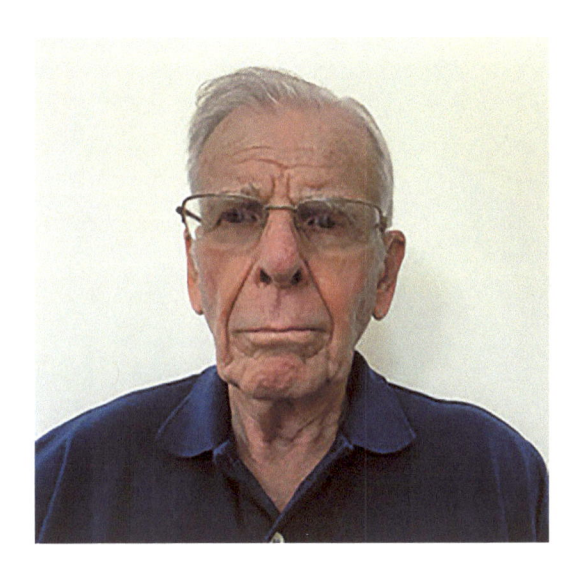